LIVING WITH ILLNESS AND DISABILITY

POISED ON THE POINTE OF PAIN

Nureyev's Foot and Other Essays

Foreword by

Her Excellency the Honourable Margaret Beazley AC KC

Governor of New South Wales

Living with Illness and Disability: Poised on the Pointe of Pain: Nureyev's Foot and Other Essays

Published by WestWords Ltd
PO Box 3708
Parramatta NSW 2124

1800WESTWORDS | admin@westwords.com.au
www.westwords.com.au

WestWords
Executive Director: Michael Campbell
Creative Producer: Ally Burnham
Associate Producer: Isabelle Quilty
Development Consultant: Kathie Elliott-Scott, Square Pegs Consulting

First published 2025

A catalogue record for this book is available from the National Library of Australia

ISBN 978-1-923044-49-4

Cover photograph: René Burri/ Magnum Photos

Graphic design by Sailor Studio
www.sailorstudio.com.au

10% of book sales will go to Chronic Pain Australia—the national voice for the 3.6million Australians living with pain.

Living with Illness and Disability: Poised on the Pointe of Pain **is supported by the Australian Cultural Fund.**

This publication is the result of a collaborative partnership between Macquarie Universtiy and WestWords

Contents

FOREWORD

Her Excellency the Honourable Margaret Beazley AC KC
Governor of New South Wales

The stories in this remarkable anthology criss-cross every human emotion – fear, sadness, despair, anger, indeed rage, bitterness, hope, more hope, joy. They bring forth every possible human reaction – disbelief, procrastination, acceptance, coping, determination, courage, compassion and the more than occasional hint of humour.

Yes, they will break your heart and yet, within a few lines, remind you of the power of the human spirit, where finding another way of living is like a rebirth, painful but joyous. Then there is the perspective of carer, who becomes the 'other side' of the bargain for which neither had intended to sign up. These are stories that needed to be written. They are stories that need to be read.

Whatever the perspective, it is precious: the dancer, whose identity and dance were one and the same – but no longer, the daughter, but no longer a daughter because dementia dictated a different story to her once loving and loved parents, the child always living with pain, always loved and encouraged to 'keep up' – but simply can't, the once strong and resilient adult, but no longer, determined not to be defined by this new and unwanted stage of life.

Putting aside medication, physio, and rehab, which are as much a duty to oneself as to others, it seems one of the few refuges for pain is the beauty of nature – the precision of the veins in a leaf or the petals of a flower, or the show of colour in a garden giving momentary relief from the intricacy and the fatigue of pain.

There is sadness, a sense of what was, and what will never be again. There are stories where memories of childhood are clung to like lichen to a cliff. The sadness comes not only in the lost opportunities, the dashed hopes, the constraints of a differently abled life, but in the lost friendships, the broken relationships, loneliness, in the grindingly slow rifts that turn into chasms of irrevocable loss – too often on both sides of a once loving relationship.

There is the reader's empathy one feels where the story is of a rare, neurological disease striking at limbs which moments before powered through doors and up stairs – a flashback to the 'polio moment' when polio struck without warning, beautifully but painfully captured in Joan London's The Golden Age. The authors have their own answers to this and the turmoil of the other imponderable questions that pain and disability toss up.

But what use is a reader's empathy in these real-life stories, one might ask? Indeed, one could ask whether empathy is helpful in any aspect of the lives of our storytellers – does one want an empathetic clinician or is it better to deal with the frank, clinical diagnosis? Is it even possible to appreciate empathy in the moment of diagnosis, pain, or treatment?

I would be remiss not to mention that there are many literary and other learned references in these stories, including to physician Dr Rita Charon, the founder and director of the Program in Narrative Medicine at Columbia University who is quoted by one of the authors as saying 'medicine has begun to affirm the importance of telling and listening to the stories of illness'. Hippocrates, traditionally recognised as the father of western medicine, would affirm that this was so, reputedly having told us nearly 2500 years ago that it is more important to know what sort of person has a disease than the disease the person has.

In providing this foreword, I have articulated many - I hope not too many - of my personal reactions to the stories in this anthology. Every author, each in their own way, whether the bearer of pain or the carer, is a hero, not because of heroic acts, because what is apparent is that there is nothing heroic about pain – but something deeply human. In giving us this anthology WestWords has exposed its readers to that deep well of humanity. It is to be congratulated.

As to the title of the anthology, I will leave that a mystery, a journey of discovery for the readers. I simply re-iterate, these were stories that needed to be told and that need to be read.

Echoes of Grace
Dancing Through Illness and Acceptance

Kathie Elliott-Scott

The morning sun casts a soft glow across my room, painting a gentle reminder of another day begun—not with the leap out of bed to pirouettes and pliés which framed my life twenty years ago, but with a cautious stretch, feeling for the edges of pain that delineate my mornings now. I lay still for a moment, allowing the memories to swirl: the bright lights, the roar of applause, the intoxicating rush of adrenaline as my body moved in time with the music, every muscle and sinew tuned to perfection. Those were my days of grace, various stages around New Zealand and the globe—from music videos to circus tents, theatre stages to stadiums, backstage with U2 and The Rolling Stones, eating snake with Cyndi Lauper, on tour with the All Blacks, partying with rock stars my body was my instrument, my art, my identity.

I was born into movement, a restless child who found her solace and expression in dance. By the age of five, clad in a yellow tutu, I was already chasing the elusive perfection of ballet, each disciplined stretch and jump a step closer to my dreams. My adolescence was a blur of rehearsals, performances, and victories—a promising talent nurtured by a beloved dance teacher who saw my potential and honed it, often waiving fees, knowing well the financial strains my single mother bore. Our life was modest, our ambitions anything but. Dance was my ticket—a way out, a way up, a way into new worlds that glittered with possibility.

Yet, at twenty-five years of age and at the pinnacle of my career, my entire world turned upside down. It was during a routine performance, completing a move I had done a thousand times before, when I felt a sharp 'ping'—a harbinger of chaos in the guise of a minor misstep. The pain was sharp and immediate, but the adrenaline of performance pushed me through. 'The show must go on,' they say, and so it did, until the curtain fell, and I could no longer ignore the agony that gripped my body.

The following months were a descent into the unknown. I couldn't walk; every attempt at movement was met by intense, searing pain and unbearable disappointment in a body that, up until then, had done so much. The journey through the medical labyrinth began with one specialist after another—surgeons, physiotherapists, neurologists, endless scans. Diagnoses were many and varied: trapped nerves, prolapsed discs, bulging discs. Treatments and therapies followed, but relief was temporary, often elusive. My life, once defined by movement, had contracted into cycles of pain management, fleeting recoveries, and frustrating relapses. Doctors struggled to understand why I wasn't healing, why the usual protocols brought no lasting improvement. Neither did the people around me understand—friends, family, fellow dancers—why I couldn't simply get better.

Years of misdiagnoses and misunderstanding culminated in a revelation two decades later when a new doctor connected the dots, presenting me with the true antagonist in my story: Ehlers-Danlos Syndrome (EDS). This diagnosis was not just a label; it was an answer, a key that unlocked the mystery of years of unexplained symptoms. Understanding EDS—a connective tissue disorder that affected everything from my joints to my digestive and vascular systems—was both a closure and a beginning. Finally, the myriad pieces of my medical puzzle fell into place, explaining the why of every unhealed injury and each inexplicable pain.

With this knowledge came a new phase of life, one not of dance, but of deep personal discovery and adaptation. No longer striving to return to the physical heights of my past, I began to explore the breadth of life within the confines of my condition. This was not the life I had planned, but it was a life nonetheless rich with potential for growth, understanding, and helping others navigate their paths through similar challenges.

After the curtains fell on my dance career, I embarked on a gruelling journey of self-discovery and adaptation. For dancers, the body isn't just a part of us; it is us. Our bodies are instruments, finely tuned and meticulously cared for, capable of expressing complex emotions and telling stories without uttering a single word. When you can no longer rely on your body, when it becomes a source of pain rather than strength, the loss is profound. It's not just the loss of physical capabilities but an entire identity built around those capabilities.

The struggle of the initial injury was daunting. After the accident, it took six months of intense physical therapy and relentless willpower just to walk unaided again. But the emotional toll of not returning to the stage was even greater. I watched from the wings as friends and former colleagues lived our shared dream—a dream that had slipped through my fingers. The feeling of being robbed, of an essential part of myself being unjustly taken away, was a spectre that haunted my every attempt to find joy in movement again.

The personal losses extended beyond the stage. During my first marriage, a brief glimmer of hope in the form of a possible pregnancy was overshadowed by a harrowing choice. The doctor warned that childbirth could confine me to a wheelchair. My ex-husband's reaction—to his credit, he was honest—was that he couldn't juggle his job, a child, and potentially a severely disabled partner. He wasn't prepared to take that risk. His certainty shielded me from confronting my own doubts or, in hindsight regretfully, seeking alternative medical opinions. The decision to have an abortion was made, which I then experienced in isolation, compounded by a profound sense of failure. No one knew. Not even my mum or dad who were both alive at the time. Society often speaks as if bearing children is a natural, effortless gift of womanhood. For me, it was a fraught battleground where my body once again betrayed me. I told people I didn't want children, a protective lie to mask the deep-seated grief of my reality.

Professionally, I redirected the drive and discipline that dance demanded into the corporate world. I excelled in sales, climbing the ranks to become the first female Regional Manager in New Zealand to run a domestic freight company. Yet, no number of professional accolades could fill the void left by my lost dance career. Each award, each promotion, was a reminder of what was truly desired and unattainable.

Interactions with others often underscored my sense of disconnection. The well-meaning 'Are you better yet?' and the myriad of unsolicited advice—from yoga to exotic supplements to massage—felt like subtle accusations, as if my chronic pain was a problem to be solved rather than a condition to be managed. The fluctuating nature of my symptoms baffled acquaintances and friends alike; I was either cancelling plans last minute or overextending myself, the latter often masked by a humour-laced reference to 'medicinal gin.'

Yet, amidst the misunderstandings, there were beacons of support. My now husband Terry, whom I met early 2018, has been my rock through every high and harrowing low. His patience and understanding have been my sanctuary; his rare frustrations never directed at me but shared with me against a world that often seems indifferent to our struggles. Conversations about 'spoons' with close friends have brought comfort and a framework to articulate the daily energy trade-offs that define living with a chronic condition. In spoon theory, a spoon represents an amount of energy. Spoonies only have a certain number of spoons per day, and have to be careful not to use more than they have otherwise they will crash.

The journey of self-reflection is often the hardest. As a former dancer whose life orbited around perfecting the self—both body and performance—the transition was jarring. My early twenties were immersed in a world where self-focus wasn't just normal; it was necessary. My first boyfriend spent hours sewing sequins on my costumes, supporting my performances, embedding himself in the arts alongside me. His sister, still one of my closest friends, remains a link to those vibrant days. Their memories of my past brilliance often contrast sharply with my present struggles, reflecting back a version of myself that feels increasingly distant.

It wasn't until I was forced out of the limelight that I confronted my own biases—internalised ableism that I didn't even recognise I had. My relentless pursuit of remedies, the backyard treatments, and the stubborn belief that I could 'fix' my disability stemmed from a deep-seated belief that without my physical capabilities, I was less valuable. As I pushed myself into various roles, trying to replicate my past successes in dance with achievements in the corporate world, I realised I was exhausting myself, not just physically but spiritually.

I constantly felt like I had something to prove. To myself, to those around me, to the world. I took on more and more work, throwing myself into each new project with the same intensity I had once dedicated to perfecting a pirouette. The promotions and awards I achieved were a temporary balm, but they never truly filled the space left by my absence from the stage. And while the world applauded my achievements in the business world, I knew that deep down, I was compensating for a loss I had never fully accepted.

My engagement with artists with disabilities just under a decade ago marked a pivotal change in my perception. Initially, I admired their resilience and saw their achievements as inspirational—external to my own experience. I saw myself as an advocate for them, a voice for their achievements, without recognising that I was one of them. This realisation wasn't immediate but evolved as I interacted more deeply within the community.

What I learned from working with these incredible individuals was that the disabled community doesn't need a voice from the outside—they have their own, potent and significant. Their narratives taught me that our society's traditional structures often sideline those who don't fit the typical mould. Being part of this community, I learned to embrace my own quirks and eccentricities, realising that these traits are not just accepted but celebrated within these circles. There's also something deeply special about finding people with the same illness as you. It's like discovering someone who shares your favourite album or movie, something so specific and intimate to you. Our shared experiences create an immediate bond, but what I treasure most is the chance to help them, to share my story, my struggles, and show them that while there may not be a fix, there's still hope.

I've come to understand the immense effort it takes to educate the public, to shift societal norms that have long been unchallenged.

The balance between educating and expressing frustration is delicate and tiring, especially when you're already dealing with daily physical challenges. Yet, this community rises to the occasion, advocating not just for personal rights but for a world where everyone, regardless of ability, can shine.

I once thought of myself as separate from this world, an ally, perhaps, but not part of it. But I was wrong. As I embraced my own disability, I realised how much I had in common with the people I had admired from a distance. It wasn't about being inspirational; it was about being seen and understood. I learned that we don't need to fit society's mould—society needs to adjust its mould to fit all of us.

However, I often feel like I'm walking a fine line between worlds. Sometimes, I feel 'not disabled enough' for the disability community, yet too sick for others. The word 'disabled' still carries such stigma for many people, and I've seen others struggle to accept that part of my identity. There are days when using the label feels like giving in, but more often now, it feels like an honest reflection of my reality. This isn't about giving up; it's about recognising that my worth isn't tied to what I can physically do. The real battle isn't within us—it's with a world that was built without us in mind. But that's changing, and it's changing because we make it so.

Adapting to life with Ehlers-Danlos Syndrome hasn't just changed how I approach work or relationships, it's also transformed my relationship with travel—a passion that's been part of me since I was young. I've always loved the thrill of exploring new cultures, experiencing different worlds, and indulging in foods I'd never even heard of before. My mum passed down her love of travel, taking me on trips to the UK from a young age, where I auditioned for and was accepted into the Royal Ballet School. Those early trips sparked something in me—a hunger to see and experience as much of the world as possible. It stayed with me through my circus days in Taiwan and my dancing tours through Asia, and it's something I refuse to give up, even with all the challenges that come with my condition.

These days, Terry often laughs about how I need to have the next holiday planned before we're even back from the current one. And though travel looks different now, we've learned to adapt, to be flexible, and to embrace the changes that inevitably come when you travel with chronic illness. There are times when plans need to shift, when rest is more important than sightseeing, and other times when you just somehow manage to dig deep and screw the inevitable consequences!

Like that day at Plitvice Lakes in Croatia in 2019. We walked 20 kilometres through the park, and though my body screamed in protest the next morning, I powered through like the Energizer bunny. It's part stubbornness, part sheer love for these moments, knowing that every adventure, every sight I get to see, is worth the pain I'll feel later. But of course, my clumsiness never lets me off the hook—falling down stairs and injuring an already fragile knee or ankle is practically a given at this point. I've become well acquainted with wheelchairs at airports, but I've learned to laugh about it. At least there's the fast lane through customs—a little perk of being a 'crip,' as I like to joke.

Another moment that really encapsulates my grit was my wedding day to Terry in April 2022 in stunning Far North Queensland. I had been diagnosed with diverticulitis and a perforated bowel just days before, but nothing was going to stop me from marrying this amazing man. I checked myself out of Cairns hospital, determined to walk down that aisle. My bridesmaid Robyn was incredible. A Kiwi, she was running around a foreign town, gathering everything I needed to stay upright and somewhat presentable, from a thermometer and hydralytes to last-minute nail polish and fake tan. My long time friend Loaine took charge of the table settings and wrangled a million little details behind the scenes, all while keeping the mood light, constantly telling me not to 'fucking die on her.' Between Robyn's patience and Loaine's no-nonsense support, I somehow managed to make it through the day. They kept me standing, laughing, and, most importantly, alive—something I'll forever be grateful for. Terry's family—my new family—just gets it. They understand I have good days and bad, and they've been nothing but supportive. I've gained not only a new mum and dad through Terry, but a sister who has faced her own health challenges with such strength and optimism. She's a rock in the family and knowing they all understand what I go through makes the challenges so much easier to bear.

My life now is all about pacing—allocating my spoons wisely, ensuring I balance energy reserves with the demands of work and relationships. Working for myself over the last decade has been a game-changer, allowing me to design my life around outcomes and deliverables rather than rigid hours. Gone are the days where 'busy' was a badge of honour. Now, I rest when I need to, plan morning appointments when I'm most focused, and prioritise energy management as carefully as I used to prioritise choreography.

Living with EDS is exhausting. My body is constantly working to hold itself together, literally. My connective tissue is lax, my joints are fragile, and my body operates without the usual shock absorbers most people take for granted. My immune system is now compromised too, thanks to a recent diagnosis of rheumatoid arthritis. And in the last few months I've also added a new condition to my crip kit bag, POTS. Postural orthostatic tachycardia syndrome (POTS) is a disorder that makes you feel faint or dizzy. It happens when the autonomic nervous system doesn't work as it should. The autonomic nervous system is the body's 'autopilot' system, controlling things like heart rate, blood pressure, and breathing. Every day is a balancing act between what I can do and what I must leave for another time. Each choice—whether to attend a meeting or cancel an event—is weighed against the cost to my body later.

Despite the challenges, I am fortunate to have an incredible support system. Terry is patient and steadfast, never showing frustration with the situation we find ourselves in. He understands what I need, often more than I do, and is there to steady me when the weight of my condition feels too much to bear. My close friends, too, have come to understand the language of spoons. Their unwavering support, despite all the last-minute cancellations and shifts in plans, has been instrumental in my ability to keep going. And yet, I often feel like a burden, wondering if they're growing tired of me, of my limitations. It's a constant battle to balance gratitude with guilt.

It's one thing to navigate your own illness but watching someone you love suffer brings a different kind of pain—one that gnaws at your heart in ways you never expect. My mum's cancer diagnosis in her early sixties shook the very foundation of my world. I had faced my own battles with my body for so long, but seeing her fight this relentless disease, I was overcome by a new wave of emotions—fear, anger, helplessness. Never before had I been so intimately connected to cancer, and it felt like I was fighting an invisible enemy on two fronts: one battle for my mum's life, and one for my own ability to cope.

I gave up my corporate job in recruitment to care for her. It felt like the only right thing to do, but as I watched her illness progress, I couldn't shake the feeling that I wasn't doing enough. No matter how many doctor's appointments I took her to, no matter how much I tried to be there emotionally, it always felt like I was failing her, failing myself. I had spent over fifteen years trying to fix my body, pushing through pain, battling to find solutions for myself—yet here was my mum, slipping away, and I couldn't do a damn thing to stop it. The frustration grew into resentment, not just for the situation but, irrationally, toward her. Why wasn't she fighting harder? Why wouldn't she help herself?

That resentment damaged our relationship in those final months. I was angry, tired, and overwhelmed. She was scared and sick. I wanted her to survive with the same desperation I'd held for myself all those years. But she couldn't, and that broke something in me. The guilt I feel from those days weighs heavy. I will always regret the moments when my frustration overpowered my compassion. She was my mum—my biggest cheerleader, my rock through all those years of dance Now, she was gone, and I was left to grapple with the void.

When she passed, the world stopped. I went through the motions—sorting through her things, handling the practicalities of death. But my internal world was in disarray. After her death, the emotional toll wasn't just about grief; it was about the constant nagging feeling that I wasn't enough. I had spent so long needing to be the best—whether as a dancer, a corporate leader, a daughter or a wife—and when I couldn't save her or myself, it felt like another failure. A few years later my first marriage broke down and it took a counsellor to point out trying to be the best at everything was driving me to exhaustion, and that maybe just being enough for myself was more important. It was then I realised I needed to find happiness within, and not in the approval of others.

Am I just a late bloomer? It feels like it's taken me so long to become the person I am today, to learn all these lessons. But maybe that's just part of the journey—figuring things out at my own pace, even if it took a little longer.

After a while, I tried to jump back into the rat race, applying for jobs, convincing myself I could go back to who I was before her illness. I landed another high-level position, but it didn't take long to realise that nothing felt the same. It wasn't just grief for my mother I was carrying; it was the culmination of years of grieving my body, my career, and the way I'd always tried to push through, to achieve and succeed, even when I wasn't truly okay.

That job was my wake-up call. It was the moment when I realised that I didn't want to keep doing this—chasing accolades, proving myself, fighting to be seen as valuable in ways that no longer aligned with who I had become. I wasn't the same person, and that was okay. It was time to stop striving for the external validations that had once driven me. I spoke to my manager, explaining my desire to start consulting and working at my own pace, helping smaller nonprofits and community organisations that didn't always have the resources or voices they deserved. I wasn't chasing a title anymore; I was searching for meaning.

It was a soft landing—my manager became my first client ten years ago, and suddenly, the future didn't seem so terrifying. I could move forward in a way that allowed me to live my truth. This new chapter wasn't about being the best; it was about doing the best I could for myself and others. I had accepted that I didn't have to be perfect, that my worth didn't depend on endless achievements. It was a slow acceptance, but it felt right.

Just six months after I lost my mum, I received the devastating news that my Step Dad had been diagnosed with the same cancer. Bowel cancer struck twice, and it felt like the universe was throwing yet another cruel challenge my way. But this time was different. I had learned from my experience with Mum. I was no longer trying to control everything, no longer demanding impossible standards from myself. I knew what to expect, and I approached my Dad's illness with a different kind of strength. I also realised that disability or chronic illness doesn't shield you from the world's hardships. We're all susceptible to life's losses, no matter what personal battles we face. I couldn't avoid the pain of both of their battles any more than I could avoid the pain of my own. It reminded me that illness doesn't separate me from others; in some ways, it draws me closer. We all have to confront suffering in different forms, but the struggle to accept, adapt, and keep going is universal.

I travelled back and forth between Australia and New Zealand, supporting him through every phase of treatment. I advocated for him with his doctors, offering insights I had gained from Mum's battle. And because I had embraced this new, flexible life as a consultant, I could work anywhere, managing my projects remotely even while sitting by his hospital bed.

When Dad passed 18 months after Mum, it was a blow, but this time, there were no regrets. I had made peace with our time together. I told him how much he meant to me, how proud I was to have had him in my life, even though he had only come into it when I was a teenager. He had been my father in every way that mattered—supporting me as a dancer, as a businesswoman, and as the person I had grown to be. His pride in me was never tied to what I achieved but simply to who I was. He taught me that, even when I doubted myself.

As I stood at his bedside, I realised how far I had come in understanding what acceptance truly meant. It wasn't about giving up on the things I had lost; it was about acknowledging that life is a series of chapters, and each one shapes us in new ways. The old me—driven, relentless, constantly striving—had been replaced by someone more compassionate, more understanding of the ebbs and flows of life. And in accepting that, I had found a deeper strength than I ever knew was possible.

Nowadays, a real win for me comes not from personal achievement but from victories for others. I've found that the most fulfilling part of my journey is helping people achieve what they thought might be out of reach, especially those in the disability and chronic illness communities. Whether it's creating the first-ever scholarship for musicians with disabilities, making music festivals more accessible, or advocating for audio description on free-to-air TV, these wins fill me with a joy that's incomparable to any accolade I once received for my dancing.

Take Booktober, for example—a campaign I started to support children's creative writing programs and provide books to under-resourced schools. Knowing that these kids have the opportunity to explore their creativity and develop their voices fills me with purpose.

I've secured funding and produced numerous projects for artists with disabilities, both nationally and internationally.

Though I can no longer dance in the way I once did, my creativity has never left me. It's just found new forms. I express myself through words now—persuasive, powerful words that are often used to bring about change. Through campaigns and fundraisers, I've channelled my creative energy into writing that matters, using language as a tool for advocacy. It's different from the fluidity of movement I once knew, but there's still a rhythm, a cadence, in crafting narratives that resonate with people and make them act.

One of my greatest desires is to delve into creative writing. I've always felt there's a story in me waiting to be written, one that goes beyond the campaign narratives I've constructed over the years. Perhaps that's my next big goal: to write fiction, to put into words all the experiences I've stored over the years.

Or maybe it's teaching dance again. My absolute dream would be to step back into a dance studio and teach, even if I can't perform in the same way. Who knows? In some world, maybe I'll be able to dance again—perhaps not in the way I once did, but in a way that suits who I am now. I'd love to attend a class again, to feel that connection to movement, even just for a moment.

But more than anything, I'd love to create a dance work that shows the beauty in difference. I want to challenge the traditional expectations of dance as a celebration of physical perfection and instead spotlight the uniqueness of every body, every movement. I want to push against the biases people have about what dance should look like and show them that grace and beauty exist in every form, whether it's through a perfectly pointed toe or the subtle sway of a body that moves differently with its own grace.

Acceptance, for me, is still a work in progress. It's not a single moment of clarity but an ongoing, ever-evolving journey. Some days, I feel at peace with where I am, with what I can and cannot do. Other days, the bitterness creeps back in, and I yearn for the days when I could leap across a stage, carefree and full of life. But I've learned that acceptance isn't about never feeling those pangs of loss. It's about recognising that it's okay to grieve what once was, while still finding joy in what is.

My hopes for the future are simple: I want to continue helping others. I want to keep showing up for the people in my life, for the artists and organisations I work with, for the disability community I'm now so proud to be part of. And I want to create art, whether through words or movement, that speaks to the truth of the human experience—the good, the bad, and everything in between.

The fear, of course, lingers. I fear that my body will deteriorate further, that one day I'll wake up and be unable to do even the small things I cherish. I fear that the people I love will tire of me, of my constant cancellations and limitations. But those fears don't define me. What defines me is the fact that, despite everything, I keep moving forward. I keep creating. I keep fighting.

I have grieved the loss of my physical capabilities, the joy of performing on stage, and the freedom that dance once gave me. But with time, I've also learned to let go of the anguish that once consumed me. I think about my birth father from time to time, about how he carried his own resentment toward the family he believed took away his music career. He gave up being a bass guitarist supporting bands like The Who and The Kinks to get married and support his family, after my mum found out she was pregnant with me, but the bitterness never left him. His grudge cast a long shadow over my childhood, and I vowed never to carry that same weight.

But when I lost dance, I felt that weight creeping in. I was angry, devastated by what had been taken from me. For years, I tried to compensate by throwing myself into work, into other forms of success, thinking that would fill the void. It didn't. And it wasn't until I stopped fighting that I realised I didn't have to live with that bitterness. My father's own resentment taught me that clinging to what's lost only poisons what's left.

Yes, I miss dance. Every day. But it's still part of my life, just in a different way. I see it in the artists I work with, in the projects I help bring to life, and in the way I've been able to channel my creative energy into helping others. The arts will always be a lifeline to me, and to so many others. Where would we be without them? It's not just about dancing or performing. It's about expression. It's about giving voice to what can't always be said. And yet, through it all, I've come to understand that perhaps the real dance of life isn't about perfect execution, but about finding grace in the moments of uncertainty.

There's one moment I keep returning to when I reflect on this journey—a conversation I had with my mum, long before she got sick, and I became disabled. She was my biggest supporter, traveling with me to competitions in our beat-up old car, sewing my costumes, cheering me on at every performance. I was on tour in Korea, exhausted and overwhelmed, when I called her from a phone box late at night. I told her how hard it was, how tired I was, how I missed home, missed her cooking, needed her cuddles. And she said to me, 'You can be tired and still love what you do. You can miss home and still be glad you're out there. But you've worked hard to be where you are, and no matter what you choose or what happens in life, you'll always be a star to me.'

That, I think, is what acceptance looks like for me. It's about holding both truths at once—feeling the loss, but also feeling the gratitude for what remains .

So, do I need to reach some final point of acceptance? Maybe not. Maybe it's enough to keep moving, to keep trying, to keep finding new ways to express who I am. Life, after all, is its own kind of dance—one that isn't about perfection, but about persistence, resilience, and the willingness to keep going, even when the music changes.

And perhaps, that's the most important lesson I've learned. The dance doesn't end when the curtain falls. It continues in the moments of quiet, in the spaces between movements, and in the ways, we choose to keep showing up, day after day, to whatever new rhythm life sets for us.

As I reflect on the journey from stages around the world to the quiet of my room, where each morning starts with testing the boundaries set by my body, I realise that grace isn't only found in the fluidity of a dancer's leap. Sometimes, grace is in the grit of facing each day with courage, in the advocacy for understanding and support, and in the embrace of a new role where my experiences lend strength to others. The echoes of my past—those glorious, flying moments—mingle with the grace of acceptance, shaping a dance of resilience that, though more grounded, is no less beautiful.

In this landscape of loss and adaptation, my life has reshaped itself around new norms—a testament to the resilience of the human spirit and the power of support and understanding from those who truly know us. As I navigate this ongoing journey, the interplay of triumph and loss continues to define the contours of my existence, always reminding me of the dance I once loved and the new rhythms I've learned to embrace.

Kathie Elliott-Scott, a former professional dancer and seasoned marketing professional with over 20 years of experience, has a strong background in arts, disability and social justice. She has secured over $15 million for projects, managed international relationships, and promoted arts and disability globally. Kathie's achievements include impactful campaigns and innovative accessibility initiatives, securing her a spot among Australasia's 'Movers and Shakers' by *F&P Magazine* in 2023.

No Longer a Daughter

On Knowing and Not Knowing Your Parents at the End.

Michelle Hamadache

Although Mum died three years after Dad, they both died in the month of May. Just as they were both born in the same hospital in Orange, my father two years before my mother. Glancing coincidences, but elegant ones that give me the sense that my parents were fated to be together. Passionate, inseparable, argumentative. Devoted. My mother was eighteen when she opened the door of the Ryde branch of what was then the Bank of New South Wales to my father. She was working on the ledger machines and Dad was the new teller with a bad-boy reputation. True to form, he arrived on his first day of work with a black eye. He'd run a betting ring during his six months of National Service and a few unhappy punters had laid into him on the train ride back the night before. He was twenty, my mother eighteen. In less than a year they were married and expecting my brother.

My father was a handsome man—tall, dark and to me at four, so much like Dean Martin that I wondered why my father's photo was on a record album, and because I adored him, I used to hold the cover of *Volare* to my chest when Dad was at work. Sometimes, I'd show guests the album so I could introduce them to my father when he wasn't at home. Dad loved it. Mum tried explaining that it wasn't Dad, but like all four-year-olds, I was good at ignoring her.

Mum was little. I was taller than her when I was ten, and though she was slim and large-breasted throughout her youth, by the time I came along, she was soft and round, and I felt myself so coterminous with her that I would do strange things like press my head between her breasts and try to push my fingers beneath her fingernails, which were red and long. She didn't enjoy me doing either of those things and was constantly trying to extricate herself from my grip, though she loved me dearly. I was born twenty-years after my first brother, eighteen years after my second, and then fifteen years after my sister. In the 1970s, when I was born, Mum and Dad were classed as old parents. In small rural towns, there was some embarrassment to be caught still having sex in your forties, or at least on not knowing better than to fall pregnant.

When I married and had children, we lived around the corner from my parents, and because of that, for a little while, my children were also my parents' children, and perhaps I remained younger than I might have done had we lived further away. These years of daily visits to my parents with one, two, then finally three children in tow, and my own childhood, are what I would like to hold onto of my parents in the glass-cased cabinet of my memory. But memory isn't a curio cabinet, it's something much more recalcitrant, more like a difficult, but passionate lover. One you can't live without, but sometimes wish you could.

My grandfather developed Alzheimer's in his late seventies, and my father had a terror of dementia. Once we drove to Crows Nest from the Northern Beaches to buy books from a cheap secondhand dealer for school. I was eleven or twelve, Dad in his fifties—fit and retired early because Westpac had restructured and no longer wanted old-style managers who had come up through the ranks from teller, to senior teller, from Grafton to Gilgandra, and back to Sydney again. He'd forgotten the list of books back home. I'll never forget him squatting in the car park, head in hands, and repeating that he'd fucken end up like his father. Dad also had plans for the 'big swim'. First signs of dementia he was heading straight out to sea. That is, even further out to sea than usual. He was a Beaches boy and swam half-way to New Zealand and back daily, rain, hail or shine. Summer and winter.

There's a while when it's difficult to tell if someone has dementia or depression, especially if there's a known history of both. Dad's uncle had blown out his brains in a semi in Ryde, and Dad, always mercurial and prone to depressive stints, especially towards the end, retreated. First from friendships, then from family gatherings, then from immediate family, and finally you could really only go and see him in his office when he asked you in. Otherwise, the door was shut, and should you open it, you'd find him glowering at you from the brown vinyl Jason recliner that had seen better days. His desk was covered in yellow post-its and lists mapping out each day from waking up to bedtime, all written and accounted for in HB pencil. His writing—every letter had a winged-tip—was strangely angular, even the letters that were meant to be round. In his seventy-seventh year he went to have some brain scans which showed he didn't have Alzheimer's. The day his results came back he was jubilant. Mum was quiet. Dad went into his office and swept all the post-its and notes into the bin. The next day they had an appointment with a geriatric psychiatrist who asked Dad to draw a clock. Mum brought it home to show me. One half of the clockface was exactly as you'd expect it to be. The other half looked like a Dali soft-clock. Dad was oblivious to the problem.

When I think about what persists about Dali's 'Persistence of Memory', it's the terrain. Land. Sky. Sea and cliff. A table. A mirror, and the emptiness. The nothingness that makes everything so sharp, everything so soft. Of course, Dali is a surrealist, but you can't unsee the pictorial version of the melting of a temporal lobe. When I close my eyes, I see a sequence. The page of a notepad with some pharmaceutical logo down the bottom. Dad's clock. Dali's clocks. Dad's clock.

It was only natural that Mum wanted to care for Dad. She grew thin again. He became voracious. Mum hid lollies and chips to try and ration them, but he'd rummage through long forgotten cupboards and find the stash. We'd go downstairs and find him with handfuls of chocolate and his cheeks bulging with mixed lollies, or in the freezer finishing off a box of Cornettos before morning tea. Once we caught him trying to eat the ornamental grapes that Mum kept on the sideboard. I suggested he might soon need to go into care. Mum replied to say that sometimes he awoke in the dead of night and grabbed her hand to tell her he thought there was something very wrong with him. They were lovers first. Inseparable.

Dad's dementia had started in the frontal lobe and then went pretty global pretty quickly. Mum refused the aged care support I'd organised because she said Dad wouldn't like being left with a stranger. The truth was she couldn't bear to be away from him, so it wasn't a surprise that Mum had a stroke, falling one morning and hitting her head on the bedside table. As though her brain was mirroring Dad's, her stroke was concentrated in the frontal lobe, like destiny. Dad's frontal lobe, Mum's frontal lobe, a hospital in Orange, both dead in May.

◆

The years since their deaths have been spent trying to forge a path through the ghastly forests of their dementias back to the time before. I haven't done a very good job of it so far. I have a sense of the things about my parents I'd like to remember, but I can't yet see past the image of my father with his rotting teeth, gaunt and bent over a book, tearing its pages from the spine, one after the other, until his feet were covered with torn paper. He was allowed to continue destroying the book because he was what they referred to as an alpha male, who would beat those he perceived as his rivals: other demented men. The male staff. Even drugged and atrophied, Dad was bigger and stronger than most of the carers. There were four clusters in his aged-cared facility. He had been moved four times to try and find a cluster that didn't trigger Dad's violent side. The management was very apologetic, but the next step was to move him out of aged care to a psychiatric ward. Fortunately, we'd agreed to palliative care, so the untreated blood clot in his calf freed itself and exploded in his heart at 11:47pm in late May 2015.

By that time, Mum was in care too. It was agreed upon by my sister and brother, nurse and doctor respectively, that it was important for her to see Dad dead. I wasn't so sure but deferred to their expertise. As though she were in a crime drama, or as if she'd mistaken the purpose of the visit for a strange exam, when shown my father, she nodded her head. 'That's him. I'd recognize that Adam's Apple anywhere.'

The stroke saved my mother from suffering. Unlike Dad whose dementia left him in a state of perpetual hell, Mum's made her into a machine. She walked, she talked, she ate, she dressed. She even moved faster after the stroke. No matter how often she was asked to slow down, to stop jogging with her walker, whether by the Occupational Therapist or me, she couldn't. She also developed a highly charged relationship with colour, creating outfits out of her wardrobe that she'd never have put together before—magenta scarfs with complex greens, a splash of electric blue thrown in. Large clip-on earrings. But she would put her trousers on back-to-front and inside out and say it didn't matter. Or she would call at 3am imperiously asking where I was and why I was late. As though I were on my own futility loop, each time she rang at that ungodly hour, I would ask her if she could see that it was dark outside. She would impatiently dismiss me. Of course she could, and what of it?

Mum's stroke took out her executive function, her temporal and spatial perception, and left her with periscopic vision—legally blind, but certain that she could see. The stroke did not take out her language centre. Articulate before the stroke, after the stroke she was razor-tongued, capable of cutting you to the quick in three or less words. Hard-hearted-Hannah was my new nickname. I'm not sure if she invented the epithet, or whether it's a maxim I'd just never heard before, whatever the case, she developed a fine sense for alliteration and stopped calling me Shelly.

I once had coffee with a friend whose mother had died decades ago, when my friend was in her twenties. I told her I didn't know what to do with this new mother. She told me she would do anything to have her mother alive. No further words about mothers were spoken, but that was the last time I saw my friend. I can't say for sure it was over our mothers, but I think it's likely. What she knew, and that I didn't say, was that I wanted my mother dead. My mother, who, when as a child I woke her up before dawn in winters in those places where outside was white with frost, would let me crawl in beside her to play Eye-Spy-With-My-Little-Eye because she'd already taught me to read. Who held me close instead of hitting me when I would scream without end and for no apparent reason though really I was too old for tantrums.

◆

I don't like Dali's 'Disintegration of the Persistence of Memory'. It's not because of the disintegration part, nor because of the way the landscape is now flooded with water as clear as glass—in fact, that I like. Especially the fish. What I don't like are those rectangular blocks. Their regularity. It offends my sensibilities. The intrusion of a techno-aesthetic into a realm that is all matter deformed. I don't care that it's now after the A-bomb, or that Dali is fascinated with science. His vision reminds me of Dad's desk with its post-it notes lined up like cards in a game of Memory. 1954 is the year Dali painted the 'Disintegration'. It's also the year that Mum and Dad married.

The day we scattered Dad's ashes, I saw him. Not like he was a ghost, but more like I was a projector. We were around at Freshwater Beach, and I decided to do some laps beforehand. As I pulled myself out of the sea-pool, I saw Dad in his navy speedos. He'd always walked like somebody comfortable naked. All dark-skin and muscle. It was warm for early winter. Maybe 21 degrees. The water temperature the same. Only the sky with that particular blue of a retreating sun. I didn't feel like I'd seen a ghost. I felt like I do when I see someone I know but they don't see me, so I can get away without saying hello. A little bit later, my brother and sister and I took turns with the dust and rubble the funeral parlor had put in a small Styrofoam esky—Dad booked his own budget funeral years before—tossing what was left of Dad out to sea. Strangely fixated on making sure we all got equal bits of Dad. Considering we've never really been the sort of siblings who share, it was anomalous behaviour. So earnest were we on the taking of turns, of watching our own hand scoop up a handful and throw, then of watching with equal attention the hand of our sibling, none of us saw the wave coming. It knocked all three of us off our feet. My brother was nearly washed off the rocks, except he landed in a rock pool just big enough for his bum, leaving his legs and torso out like he was in some kind of a barrel. My sister and I dropped to our knees and gripped, knees and palms sliced on barnacles. The bloody photo taken of the three of us shows us each jubilant, my sister in the middle with the empty esky facing the camera. Job done. And Dad got us all one. Never take your eyes off the sea. That was the mantra we grew up with.

Mum ended up in the suburb of Marks Point with my sister. Mum didn't really know how to swim, so never wanted to be scattered in the ocean. She wanted a rose in the Crematorium, but unlike Dad, she didn't research it. It costs $14,000 to have one of those plots. Although there was consensus among my siblings that Mum would hate us spending that on a plot for ashes that no one would visit—we weren't brought up to visit the dead—so my sister picked up the ashes, and took them home, burying Mum under a rose bush in her garden.

Dad's suffering made him tragic. His knowing and not knowing were inextricably bound, like the nucleus of an atom. Even in his most tortured moments of forgetting he was still retaining some dark current of knowing the snare. Mum's dementia created a parodic version of a woman who kept love alive through fifty-nine years of marriage with a man who drank too much and a son who smashed himself to smithereens at nineteen. A woman who moved twenty-seven times in forty-five years, mostly to shitty little towns with populations under four digits and with fifty degrees variation in temperatures between summer and winter.

The cruelty of a parody is that it wounds the original. In the case of my memory of mum, perhaps fatally. It was Oscar Wilde who pointed out how deficient life is in form. Its comedies grotesque. Its catastrophes happening in the wrong way to the wrong people. Life always goes on too long, or not long enough. A beginning, a middle and an end. Memory=projector=metaphor. Some kind of causality between events. Perhaps a fracturing of story to subvert these things. A canopy of days. Nights that stretch across the forest floor. Years that fall apart like leaves shook loose from some more enduring structure. Faces that appear and disappear in dappling light. Parts of my parents' dementias were incorporated into the architecture of my mind. This sense still that the garish light of a flickering projector superimposes recency over primacy; the longer it runs, the less of my parents as they were that I have. The irony that so much of what I've lost is the stuff of memory, as though I have my own specific form of dementia. A dementia-induced dementia.

It's likely I won't mourn my parents. According to Freud, I would need to be able to meet their absence in each of the places I would once have met their presence. But the way things stand, that would mean conjuring the ghouls of their dementias, and then concentrating hard—perhaps with props and assistance from those who knew and loved them too—in order to reanimate them again as my parents. And only then to have them vanish, like ghosts extinguished, all to mourn them properly. A danse macabre I have neither time nor inclination to perform. What I do have is form. The way I know to rise in the morning and put the day on like a freshly ironed shirt. No matter what. For a little while longer to play a member of the masked chorus in a tragedy whose ending is written every day. Not tragedy as it is used so flippantly, with cliché and ubiquity, but tragedy as a form that relies on a world that shuffles the cards of fate and silence, gods and knowing, objects and ignorance, and sometimes hubris and gore to produce a feeling, on occasion, called transcendence.

Then there is the grotesque. A bending of the natural order to give tortured faces to walls and trunks with roots to human torsos. Dali's camembert clocks. What humans have done to say what can't be said. My mother the automaton became the perfect figure of the grotesque, both living and somehow not. A fast-moving flesh-machine. When I try to find a language for how I live with the fact I am no longer a daughter, there is company and comfort in these forms that have surely have known the impossibility of order and meaning longer than me. And in the coincidence that Mum and Dad, who once shared a nursery in a small rural hospital of a town neither of them lived in again, met again, and loved and lived, and then died in May of wounded brains that I imagine as thin-sectioned. The two halves of a Rorschach butterfly.

Michelle Hamadache is Director of Creative Writing at Macquarie University. She writes essays, short stories and reviews and has had publications in US, UK and Australian journals. She was fiction reader and editor at *Southerly* and an editor at *Mascara Literary Review*.

The War Within

Jacqueline Greig

By the time Covid struck, I was a veteran. A veteran of fighting for the recovery of my patients; the battles my medical training had taught me to fight. I was also well versed in grappling with personal health skirmishes, those for which no textbook exists. Dog-eared, med-student texts had instilled the knowledge that white blood cells and antibodies rage against invaders as fiercely as on any battlefield, but it took my CIDP to teach to me how painful that raging can be. When Covid commenced its unstoppable circumnavigation of the globe, I already understood illness as the messy business of war.

The virus not only locked us inside to escape its reach but forced us to look outside, beyond our borders, beyond ourselves. This strange, spiky creature had everyone talking about DNA and RNA, the replication and recombination of nucleotide strands. Notoriously boring medical specialties, like immunology and epidemiology, became glamourised medical detectives hunting the dangerously mutating Corona virus as it evaded our immune systems. Mutants—creatures previously only populating the war-torn, celluloid realm of the Marvel world—were among us, forcing everyone to swot up on the Greek alphabet, grasp basic cell division, and understand the importance of spike proteins. Those protruding bits that help the virus resemble a tumbleweed but are indeed the key to unlocking our cells. This ever-changing spike protein must be recognised as foreign by our immune system on its search and destroy missions against Covid19. Mutation during a pandemic is not only war but evolution at dizzying speed.

Some ten years earlier, when my auto-immune illness, Chronic inflammatory demyelinating polyradiculoneuropathy—CIDP, struck, I had been completely unprepared for war. Apt or ironic, I experienced the first, terrifying symptoms on one of my family's beloved museum trips. It was a presage of what would replace my happy life of ordered-chaos as mother-doctor with more pain, fear and loss than I could have believed possible. In those halls where evolution is laid bare, my genetics, my evolution, my CIDP caught up with me.

My sons, Chris, Cam, and Patrick stood clustered before Archaeopteryx, the earliest discovered fossil link between dinosaur and bird. My eyes traced the primordial feathers and hollow bone structure that had been embedded into fine-grained limestone some 150 million years ago. The boys wondered whether this was a dinosaur-bird or a bird-dinosaur. Like many children, mine were obsessed with dinosaurs and the basics of Darwin's Evolutionary Theory. Nature as cruel winnower, removing the chaff to allow the strongest, the healthiest, or the best adapted, to survive.

To humanity's detriment, evolution is portrayed as constant improvement, when in truth, evolution is frequently content with mediocrity. The more specialised a species, the more vulnerable it becomes. In Africa, where I grew from child to young adult, lives the long-tailed widowbird. In spring, the male produces an enormous, black-feathered tail that it flaunts together with its bright red and yellow wing epaulettes. This feathered splendour entices the drab, inconspicuous female; and in her choice of mate-most-glorious she perpetuates ever more sartorial tyranny upon the males.

I would watch the male birds laboriously flapping against the mildest breezes to reach where the females nested, and I wondered how they survived. As an adult, I learned that many don't—the male birds are indeed irresistible, easy prey to sharp eyed raptors circling above. The kind of spectacular sexual dimorphism displayed by widowbirds during the breeding season comes at a long-term survival cost for the species.

Evolution, like science, is double edged, often not a race to perfection but the best fit for the situation. With time, I would come to more fully comprehend that survival is a tangled game of getting by. There in the museum, in the moment when my legs gave way, my arms tingled, and my heart raced, this learning began. In sudden and terrifying ways CIDP had arrived to rule my body.

In the acute care hospital, I lay immobile, narcotic stupefied, from January to March 2010. When the most painful of my symptoms had been controlled, it would take another six months in the rehabilitation unit before I arrived home in a wheelchair.

Spring preceded my homecoming and had clothed the grevilleas in pink and ruby-gold, familiar friends that nodded wiry heads in welcome. A warm, silky afternoon that echoed with the call and response of whipbirds. There was awkwardness in returning to a place not lived in for so long. The children's initial joy settled, and my partner stopped asking if I needed another coffee, turning again to his newspaper and work. His life already irrevocably altered too.

I couldn't walk without aides and tired easily. My previously rapid, easy movements were now stiff, erratic, and dangerously clumsy. CIDP is an unrelenting puppeteer, a cruel puller-of-strings that would move my limbs without my consent. A master who resisted with astonishing strength any of my attempts to move. I had become as wooden a marionette as Pinocchio and equally as poorly equipped to face the world. This disability, which had commenced as a terrifying torrent over which my husband and I reached to clasp hands, had by now carved an inaccessible canyon between us. The treacherous walls of this divide threw my words and thoughts back to me. How empty the sound of one's own thoughts. Pain in loneliness and loneliness in pain. Love does not always endure; ours now a schism without hopes of reconciliation.

I found no way of repairing the rent torn between us. None of the tales and truths that formed the connective tissues of my childhood family, who had stayed together despite wars, illness, personal desires, had equipped me for this painful separation. I kept circling back to family inheritance, the stories we carry, and the medleys of luck buried in our genes, some DNA a gift, some a curse.

◆

CIDP is an autoimmune disease, which means the body's immunological defence system turns upon and devours the self. In CIDP, the rogue immune system targets nerves outside the brain: the peripheral nerves that control physical action and sensation. Without these nerve tendrils our haptic, kinetic experiences are erased. CIDP is a thief that steals your agency.

The genesis of autoimmune diseases, these destroyers-of-self by a system designed to protect, is intriguingly bound to evolution. What Covid failed to teach us, due to the rapid production of effective vaccines, is that infectious diseases exert strong, selective evolutionary pressures. Superficially it seems that infections carry away the old and the weak, leaving a stronger gene pool to survive and thrive. However, being random rather than linear, evolution leaves gaps and quirks in the web it creates.

The Black Death that killed at least 30% of the Afro-European population during the Middle Ages exposes such an evolutionary gap and a link to autoimmune disease. During that epoch the existence of a bacteria with a complicated rat-louse-human lifecycle could not have been fathomed. That the devastating sickness was caused by a microscopic, safety-pin shaped organism called *Yersinia pestis* would only be discovered four hundred years later. Further understanding has recently, literally, been unearthed. Analysis of DNA within skeletal remains from before, during, and after the plague shows that if your DNA contains a codon known as ERAP2, then your chance of surviving *Yersinia pestis* is 50% greater than a non-carrier. That's good, you think, I hope I own that little group of nucleotides. Don't be too hasty! This sequence of nucleotide building blocks controls part of our complex immune system. The flipside of ERAP2: it significantly increases the risk of developing autoimmune diseases like rheumatoid arthritis, systemic lupus, and CIDP. The powerful immune response that saved our ancestors from the Black Death now renders us vulnerable to risk of internal attack. The path from ancestor to us winds atop a precipice.

◆

During those long, bed-bound, hospital months, I would awake each day to recall that I had tumbled from that genealogical precipice. Once back at home my reduced body was placed on the veranda with a book, a cup of coffee, and circling thoughts. A tiny world. Hands too numb and clumsy to wheel the chair. A dependent world. Asking to be pushed from bathroom to bedroom to kitchen. An endless loop of need.

From the verandah the land dipped down towards where the bush began, where silver-green eucalypt branches tossed, restless and shimmery. There a wallaby and her dark baby grazed, gentle, nervous-eyed creatures that bounded away into the terpene-scented shade of the forest at the slightest disturbance. The trees sheltered birds in multitudes of colour and clamour. Avian couples readying for another season's pairing, nest building, and brooding. Come summer, their young would emerge as smaller, duskier versions of their parents, fledglings questing to be fed while exhausted adults willed them to forage for themselves. The habit of nurturing dies hard.

On school mornings, my boys would dash into my patch of sunshine to hug me goodbye and then leave an aching silence that flooded every corner. Even the daily arrival of Annie, the housekeeper-carer hired to help me, who diligently cooked and cleaned, brought what I needed and helped me to bed when sleep called, did little to ease my grief. I had come adrift, detached from the world.

My children became free and feral. Most Saturdays, they merged like small wallabies into the bush. They returned hours later having dug through the shale pile, encountered goannas, watched water dragons, or glimpsed the resident diamond python curled on his rocky ledge—a sinuous creature who observed them with brown-gold eyes and tongue flicks, tasting the air. On their return, the boys would throw their young bodies, still fragrant with the tang of eucalypt and tea-tree, upon me. Patrick and Cameron, with solemn fingers, delineated a fossil they saw in a shale fragment, while Chris draped his newly lanky body on a bench nearby, hazel eyes narrowed against the harsh light. A few brief, bright moments to hold these youngsters in my heart.

Weekdays, when I wasn't at rehab, I had the company of birds: peewees in pied overcoats pecking hopefully around my chair; the momentary emergence of a shy whipbird; an amorous king parrot couple preening with gentle chirps and high, clear whistles. The parrots eventually flitted away, besotted synchronicity, a shimmer of scarlet-green.

I had always loved wild birds: a girl enthusiastically taking charge of the binoculars on African Highveld walks and pouring over avian identification texts. After migrating to Australia, this continent's abundance of brilliant, raucous parrots only increased the fascination.

Affinity for nature is multifactorial, anthro-zoological studies suggest it to be partly genetic, but for my two brothers and me the experience of Africa's creatures and Oma Lili's stories greatly contributed.

For six weeks of each year, our Dutch-Indonesian grandmother, Oma Lili, would visit. It was a long trip from her hometown of Ruurlo in the Netherlands to our sun-soaked, African childhood. When Oma visited, our home echoed with laughter and we ate *Nasi Goreng*, *Gado-Gado*, and *Rjis Tafel* spiced scorching hot with *sambal-oelek*. Decorative bowls of chopped *pisang* and salted *pindas* graced the table. Where did mother store those bowls when Oma Lili wasn't there?

After our evening meal, Oma gathered her grandchildren into her softness and told us stories, myths and truths. Born on the island of Java, Oma spoke the lore of verdant islands that had been the source of her bedtime stories growing up in Batavia (Djakarta).

Then, I didn't know of her pain as she never mentioned the war; only spoke of islands whose indigo skies and geometrically terraced hillsides she longed to return to. The Moluccas and the Greater and Lesser Sundas of the Indonesian archipelago scatter across the ocean like a handful of carelessly tossed emeralds.

But Oma's nostalgia for her place of birth and youth was blotted with unimaginable horrors of war. Occasionally, I puzzled at how easily her batik-blue eyes could fill with tears. A child believes this is weakness; most of us will learn it is strength. The nature of that strength would unfold as my own medical imprisonment led me back to her words. Pages from her diaries, words for decades caught between worn and faded covers, never quite forgotten. Oma had gifted us written memories and tales told.

'Koka bird sings *ku-kau ku-kau*,' Oma would start an evening tale. 'He's bald and wrinkled because at time's beginning, he quarreled with Rawa bird. In those long-distant times, Rawa wanted dark and light to take turns each year. Imagine that!' she'd stop, wide-eyed. 'How many, many hours would you have to spend at school on such a day?'

Silently, her grandchildren considered this impossibility.

Rawa insisted that people should live forever, but wise Koka believed that night and day should be short, that people could not live forever, but rather make children to replace them when they left this earth. Stubborn Rawa believed that seven people would be enough to fill the earth, that a single grain of rice could overflow a cooking vessel, and that fields need only be planted once to produce rice forever. The two birds shrieked and squawked, until, losing all patience, Koka hurled a pot of black batik dye at Rawa. Horrified by the dark streaks on his previously pearl-white feathers, Rawa roared in anger and threw scalding porridge over Koka's head and neck. The porridge burned the tender skin and feathers leaving terrible scars.'

She always paused here to sip tea while we absorbed this peculiar fight. Perhaps she was momentarily transported back, not to mythical times, but to the violence they portend.

'The fabled 'People of the Horizon', who had been watching the argument, hurried over to calm ruffled and singed feathers. Being powerful godlike creatures, they declared that day and night should quickly follow each other, and that humans should love and enjoy children. 'Which,' Oma would add, 'is why you are here listening and know, that from then on, wise Koka bird greets the dawn, and as the sun sinks toward the horizon, pied Rawa bird chants the evening into night. Those stubborn creatures still haven't learned to talk to each other.'

I have since discovered that Koka and Rawa are Australasian birds that migrate from Indonesia to Australia over summer. I believe Oma Lili would have recognised them, but she never visited Australia or learned their antipodean names. We call Koka the Noisy Friar Bird or, colloquially, Old Leatherhead. A wrinkled, bald creature with its blackened beak, certainly the most ungainly of Australia's ubiquitous Honeyeaters. Koka is called Wirgan in the Eora language of the Sydney sandstone country where I put down roots some years after arriving in Australia. Frequently these gargoyle birds raided the garden's Lili-pilis for nectar, their scolding gossip reaching my veranda vantage point.

Rawa are Pied Imperial Pigeons, the legend of the catastrophic black ink captured forever on their feathers. I didn't see them often but occasionally heard their soft, cooing plaints and the sensual ruffling of their breast feathers at dusk.

Birds helped me cope with time's slow tick, a previously unknown sensation, of hours to fill, days to spare, and long weeks looming. Time had become tortuous. I escaped into the past fearing my future of numb hands and feet, of feeling encased in a skin-shell, a life too hideous and exhausting to figure or fight. I became an archivist piecing together stories, fusing memory and present adversity. Our family's war, blood-stained and personal, was written in Oma's hand. Letters and diaries that I'd not had time for until now.

I discovered that Oma's feathered creation myth of cyclical renewal was a pastiche drawn from several islands of the Indonesian archipelago. Recalling scraps of the original telling, she stitched them into coherency. Her whole life had been the taking of little and making much, a tale of loss from war's incoherent violence followed by slow restoration.

The elegant, Dutch cursive of Oma's diary revealed a theatre of cruelty, healing, and surviving. The stories Oma had never told were at my fingertips; the words evoked her voice; the sentences on the faded pages immersed me in her life. Some parts were more love letters to her absent husband than diary. There were snippets about the health of their children, but also heartbreaking news of friends vanished and later found with heads severed from their bodies. She circled from tragedy back to small joys and persistent faith.

Reading her diary would become my daily ritual, preventing me from drifting into despair. Each day Oma emerged from the pages, taking my hand, and walking me into her cool, shadowy domain. I could hear tinkling from the piano that stood upright against the wall of the voorkamer. I smelled the sweet jasmine scent of the melati vine and believed I heard the voices of my ancestors.

Number 22 Kwitang Jalan, Weltevreden, my Oma and Opa's home, stood near Batavia' s canal network, the Dutch-colonial channels of the great, winding Tjiliwoeng (Ciliwung) River, which still shapes modern day Djakarta. Canals where women hung washing on crisscross bamboo frames and children played in tropical heat.

The rear garden of the cream-coloured house abutted a sprawling kampong, a maze of alleys between *alang-alang* (thatch) roofed homes and market gardens thrumming with humanity. The front of Number 22 was screened from the road by enormous palm trees and a bamboo façade. Oma and her siblings, like the preceding generation, had been born in that house. A genealogical mixture of Indonesian-Dutch, called *Indos*[1], they felt one with the bustling city and the distant, terraced hills. Descendants of colonizers and Indonesians, intermarriage leading to a mingling and merging of genes, they spoke Malay and Dutch with equal fluency. For a child to question this belonging would be to question her existence. Oma had never seen the Netherlands with its flat, low horizon and enormous cloud-sky. She did not know the touch or taste of snow. Like her mother before her, Oma watched her children grow through heat and monsoon downpours.

My father, Emile, was a blond-headed, black-eyed boy of six when, two weeks after the fall of Singapore, the warplanes arrived. Planes, wing roundels shining with the rising sun, whirling in dogfights against the Royal Dutch Air Force and their British, American, and Australian allies. Emile, and older brother Jan, fascinated rather than frightened, often left the air raid shelter to watch, meticulously identifying each plane's insignia and type. My father's fascination with planes would never wane; as children, my brothers and I would visit the airport with Dad to identify airline tailfin logos. On one such occasion Dad told me that for him, the war truly began the day his Papa came home in khaki KNIL (Royal Netherlands East Indies Army) uniform. Papa's warm tobacco-and-starch hug engulfed his small son and filled Emile with fierce pride. But Papa gave no hint of how poorly prepared the Dutch were for the coming storm.

---

[1] *Indische-Nederlanders, Indo-Europeans:* In 1930, given the long history of colonisation of Indonesia, first by Portuguese, then Dutch, close to 50% of Europeans living in Indonesia were 'Native Eurasians' known as Indo-Europeans, or simply, Indos.

A few days later, on March 5, Batavia was occupied by the Japanese, a city now shadowed by acrid smoke billowing from burning oil reserves at Tanjong (Tanjung) Priok Harbour. On March 9 the Dutch surrendered and for the first time Oma felt her inclusion slipping away: being Indo suddenly meant belonging nowhere. The invaders put the *Tolok* (Dutch) in camps, but the *Indo* 'half-breeds' confounded them. How to categorise such people, where to put them, even how to torture them? Belonging would become an ominous numbers game of age and *asal-usal*, (genetic origin). My Opa was taken away to Changi and then the Thai-Burma railway, the family was imprisoned at home, rather than the camps for Dutch women and children. Home familiar, yet terrifying, as soldiers patrolled, entered, damaged, searched, threatened.

The conquerors had swaggered in on promises of Indonesian freedom and independence but marched out with war requisites of oil and rubber. Japanese concerns lay primarily with their war effort, they recruited Indonesians to work on railways as far away as Burma. People, initially willingly, then forcibly, were recruited soon finding themselves exploited, beaten, and starved. Families of these *romusha*[2] were left without their men, without food, without hope. As the war limped on, the US submarines tightening their noose around the Japanese Pacific fleet, a tenuous situation became increasingly dire.

Behind its foliage, 22 Kwitang, strove to avoid prying eyes of patrolling soldiers and visits from traitorous officials. Its relative invisibility allowed it to function as a school, medical-clinic, radio-communication outpost, and occasional bolt hole.

On weekdays, a small group of pupils filed into a row of desks hidden behind the rear wall of the house. In hushed tones they bid Miss Lili, 'Goeden morgen,' and lessons commenced. My Oma Lili was determined that invasion would not impede education. Determined to teach in Dutch, not Japanese, as proscribed by the oppressors. She refused to learn this language of war, a refusal which could have cost her life.

---

[2] *Romusha:* Japanese word meaning 'labourer' however, during the war rapidly coming to mean 'forced labourer'.

From her diaries, her determination and humour leapt from the page. I delighted in the scribbled asides, jotted verisimilitudes between Dutch and Japanese with which she wickedly taunted the soldiers. After all these years, it dawned on me that Oma hadn't been speaking Japanese as purported, when, in serious tones she reeled off, 'Sapporo Yokohama Tokyo Takayama Osaka,' to her admiring grandchildren who didn't know Japan's geography.

Her writing recorded devastating events in painful clarity, yet the words seemed to bring release. Entries beginning in sombre tones but ending with touches of levity, her pen dispelling the sorrows of war. In reading her words, her release became mine too.

She repeatedly reassured her husband, or perhaps herself, that they would be together again. Her faith and fearlessness in the face of the invading army, so at variance with my constant anxiety. Mine a fear of the invasion happening internally, of being overwhelmed by an army within. To be forsaken, even attacked, by oneself bred a paralysing anxiety.

I struggled to overcome that fear every day, feeling that if I gave up, my body would be overwhelmed. In a strange simulacrum I, like Oma, needed to make do with little: if my few remaining nerves didn't stimulate the muscles, they would atrophy and disappear. I needed every left-over muscle fiber, every myosin-actin tendril interaction, to rebuild my movement. Oma used language to sustain her; I used each muscle contraction.

Oma's pages told of Anneke, her practical, older sister, whose family lived in the labyrinthine, hidden house too. Anneke, though not a nurse, started a small clinic using medical skills she'd learned assisting her husband, Dokter Victor, in his surgery. Skills he would never know she used so frequently and expertly. The trauma of war, like the trauma of illness, clasps the hand of medicine.

After the fall of Singapore, Dr Victor had volunteered as a ship's doctor. His name is listed on the manifest of the re-purposed merchant vessel the *Poelau Bras*[3] as 'Officer of Health' with the Dutch Marine

---

[3] The most well-known survivor of the sinking of the *Poelau Bras* was Helen Colijn, who wrote about her experiences in *De Kracht van Een Lied*, later translated as *Paradise Road: Song of Survival* and produced into the movie *Paradise Road* in1997.

Corp. On board were families fleeing from *Tjilatjap* (Cilacap) in Java to Columbo in Ceylon (Sri Lanka) during the desperate days before the formal surrender of the Netherlands to Japan.

Victor must have had an inkling of the risks, the tally of already destroyed ships, bombed as they sailed with women, children, wounded soldiers, and civilians, fleeing Singapore and Indonesia. However, it would be years before the truth, that fewer than twenty percent of these merchant ships made it to safety, was revealed.

Only hours from reaching the open ocean, and safe passage, the roar of Japanese planes filled the skies above the *Poelau Bras*. Merciless strafing and bombing mortally wounded the ship, a craft overburdened with 260 people, five times greater than her usual load. Water rushed through the vessel's gaping wounds. The air filled with groans of the dying ship and screams of passengers trapped between flooded decks or incinerated by the inferno above. Only three lifeboats, with hundred and six survivors, escaped the rapidly submerging wreck.

Victor surely clung to the memory of his wife and children through the seven, hot, exhausting days before his lifeboat reached Belimbang (Vlakkenhoek) lighthouse on the southern point of Sumatra.

It is known that he arrived ashore, and treated several wounded survivors for some days, before, he and two colleagues set off to find help on foot, knowing that Japanese soldiers were taking no prisoners. No trace of the three men has been found.

Anneke knew of Victor's arrival at Belimbang and sustained by fierce hope she filled the days treating those who asked for help at the door of Kwitang 22.

The history of war is punctuated by huge events and tectonic shifts, but for those living the war, its days are filled with the small and personal. This is no less heroic; all battles are ultimately our own.

Occasionally, as I held my own children and explained how my illness hurt, I quailed at how Anneke must have felt when her four-year-old daughter asked when Papa would come home from the war.

My father had told me war stories, broken memories of his childhood, certain incidents recalled vividly, while others, too terrifying, had fled to inaccessible recesses of his mind. And I, the listener, was left feeling disconnected and unsynchronized, catching at fragments spooling away from me like snippets on a cutting room floor. Now, Oma's diary pieced the fragments into coherence.

Oma wrote of the early days occupied with gardening, the planting of vegetables, and acquiring hens to lay eggs for precious protein.

The digging of their potato patch unearthed a treasure. Oma's tense, scribbled description evoked the anxious beat of her heart, and it seemed as if I too heard that long-ago shovel strike and the sound of dirt scraped from a muddy box. The collective intake of breath and tense murmur as the lid was pried loose. No glittering treasure or pile of sovereigns but, glinting in the morning sun, lay rows of silvery fluid vials, pill bottles, empty syringes, and rolled bandages.

Had the absence of a pirate hoard disappointed the child my father was? Perhaps he had run to hide in his favourite spot, under the sweet-scented jasmine at the garden's end. A scent forever reminiscent of incarceration and yet always soothing. Remembered beauty, repressed pain.

Did the adults finally search for him or did itching mosquito bites drive the boy inside? Whatever happened, he certainly came to understand the poignant significance of the find: it would not only save his life but many others.

The box and its contents would prove more valuable than any conventional treasure. Sulphur pills, penicillin, vitamins, bandages and antiseptics, all hurriedly buried by Victor before he boarded the fateful ship. He knew that war creates desperate needs and feared the medicines would be snatched by the invaders. But he could not have foreseen, as he dressed in his naval uniform and hugged his family goodbye, holding his youngest against his clean-shaven face and drawing her sweet baby smell into his memory, that the medicines would be his last gift to them.

I once heard a Homeric chant, a string plucked melody telling of Apollo, god of healing, curing Ares, god of war. 'As fig-juice, pressed into bubbly, creamy milk, curdles it firm for the man who churns it round, so quickly he healed the violent rushing Ares.'[4] Now, I understood that, as Apollo had healed Ares, so war and medicine are always dangerously, inextricably, entwined.

Oma did not record medical facts, preferring to tell of people, their strength and, occasionally, their suffering. She dwelt on the personal, not the clinical. In her slanted handwriting, I read a name I recognised—Intan—and the date he came to their door begging Anneke for help. His name recalled my father's recount.

'The war brought increasing desperation for all Indonesians,' my father had said. 'Hill families came to the city to find work and food, but there was nothing for them, many starved by the roadside. Mama seldom let me leave the house, she knew I would see people of skin-and-bone, hopeless and helpless. Once I saw a person lying, unmoving in the mud, I knew I saw a corpse.' Dad would shudder before continuing, 'One morning a young man knocked at our door. Thin and too weak to support himself, he staggered rather than walked. I filled with horror at seeing maggots crawling through the flesh of his legs. I glimpsed ivory-white bone beneath his ravaged muscle. Anneke put Intan into a bed in one of the front rooms, where we children weren't allowed. She cleaned and dressed his weeping leg ulcers. He was fed and administered thiamine, a vitamin from the treasure chest. Beriberi was common; Anneke easily diagnosed and treated it.'

'Intan's recovery fascinated my brother and me—I because it felt miraculous, my brother because he wanted to become a doctor. It took six weeks for Intan to walk and three months before he was well enough to leave us.' Here, Dad paused, as if not wanting to finish, or perhaps wishing he could leave it at this. But he had lived when war and science clashed.

---

[4] The Iliad, Book 5, lines 1045-107. God of war Ares receives treatment on Mount Olympus for his battle wound from the god of healing Apollo, on orders of Zeus.

'The saddest part of this story,' he would continue with a sigh. 'Is Intan's returning a year later, again afflicted with beriberi. Anneke couldn't help him. There was no thiamine left among the silver vials.'

The symptoms of dry beriberi or acute nutritional polyneuropathy mirror CIDP, both chronic polyneuropathies stripping myelin from nerve sheaths: leaving skin a numb carapace and gait clumsy, precarious, ataxic, wide-based. Monthly immunoglobulin infusions keep me alive; a decent diet was all Intan would have needed.

Like the seasons of Australia's Northern Territory, beriberi exists as the Wet and the Dry. The dry form is neurological while beriberi's wet form causes heart failure. This condition, previously known as 'dropsy', derived an ancient Greek word *hydrops,* that means 'accumulation of water'. When the heart fails, the body's tissues clog with fluid leaking from stagnant blood vessels. Without thiamine treatment, both wet and dry beriberi are deadly.

Beriberi's history is of perceived progress and colonialism's devastating reach. A previously rare condition, it rapidly spread through Asia during the nineteenth century, a time when Nobel laureate Robert Koch's germ theory of illness predominated. Thus, it was believed a mystery germ floated in the miasma of the rice fields and, as long as the pathogen remained elusive, beriberi would spread misery and death.

Then, Dr Christiaan Eijkman's chickens came to the rescue. While working in the Javanese port town of Tjilatjap (Chilacap), surrounded by paddy fields and overlooking the emerald waters of Schilpadden Baai (Turtle Bay), the young doctor noticed his chickens drunkenly staggering and tremulously staring skywards before succumbing to immobility. Eijkman knew beriberi when he saw it and was amazed to discover that feeding the chickens brown rice, rather than the leftover white rice from the kitchens, was curative.

Milled, polished rice has longevity and improved flavour. As imperial powers spread across Asia, laborious hand-pounding of rice was replaced by mechanical milling. While traditional pounding removed only the rice husk, the milling machines removed both husk and thiamine-rich germ. This 'germ-free' rice spread beriberi across Asia.

Although scientists had already coined the term vital-amine, and even identified thiamine by 1936, thousands upon thousands of people in Southeast Asia and the Japanese POW camps suffered from, or died of, beriberi. Prisoners, my grandfather and uncle among them, were fed almost exclusively cheap and easily stored, polished white rice. A terrible triumph of expediency.

Dusk, some six months after my homecoming I closed the diary for the day as a boobook owl's plaintive refrain hung on the darkness. It seemed the verandah thronged with ghosts, chimeric ghosts entwining DNA, history and mythology. Events, previously sepia, were becoming part of me, Oma's words brought past and future, illness and war, myths and truths, together much as they had when I was a young girl listening at her feet.

There would be more pages to read and more people to know. The diary still helping me survive and understand loss and gain.

Tomorrow, another infusion and another two hours at the rehabilitation hospital. Tomorrow, my mother, finally granted a three-month visa, would arrive.

As the weeks unfolded, my physiotherapist mother, walked with me distances lengthening by a few, slow, painful steps each day. She massaged my aching limbs and Patrick, my son with thistle-down hair, begged her to help. My body cried for my stolen sensations. Touch, frequently excruciating in its new, strange sensory manifestations, would always remain my addiction, a hunger that never leaves.

Oma's words and my mother's actions lifted my despair. Mom held my children when exhaustion denied me the task. My recovery would be slow, not the rushed healing of Ares, nor Anneke's near-miracle healing of Intan; and, like Intan, cure would never be complete, nor assured.

The body is hostile as any warzone when it turns upon itself, but inheritance is not merely a series of genes, a string of nucleotides; it's also a long-strung legacy of shared stories from which to draw strength and healing.

Jacqueline Greig has lived several lives. She has worked as a country GP, a city Obstetrician, and is mother to three boys. For the past fourteen years she has grappled with CIPD, a neurological condition with protean manifestations. Jacqui completed her Masters in Creative Writing with Macquarie university in 2022. Her literary passion is creative non-fiction in which she can explore nature, science, medicine, the past and the future. She received the Dean's award for excellence for her Masters thesis *Out of Touch: Losing Nerves and Natures Networks*.

It's in the Beat

Penny Macoun

I was born without a pulmonary artery or pulmonary valve. The operations to repair this when I was a child caused so much internal scarring that my heartbeat went awry, meaning that I need an internal defibrillator to keep me alive.

I also have a wandering eye. You'd be surprised by how many people have asked, 'Why aren't you looking at me?' As though it's something I can control. I also can't drive, and I walk with a long cane. When I was a child, I was legally blind, but through work with a developmental optometrist and the use of reading glasses, I am now borderline for driving. But at 45, I won't bother now.

Anyway, with the CHD—short for Congenital Heart Disease—the defibrillator, the Tracheal Stenosis, mental health issues, the Nystagmus and other vision impairments, I tend to just tell people I am 'A Biological Screwup' and change the subject. Sometimes it gets a laugh.

I have learnt to make jokes. I have to. You can imagine the judgements I have received, the looks, the condescending questions. I was once told by a guy on eHarmony that no guy would want to go out with me because I don't have the stamina to keep up with him. He would appear to be both horrid and right. I am the only one in my entire family and friends that is still completely single. No partner or children, and a lot of that is due to the CHD and other medical conditions.

◆

I have disjointed memories of Cardiologist appointments, and having chest x-rays, which I would have to take with me each time I saw him. I remember these moments more like photos, I know they happened, but I could not say when. I asked my Mum if she was aware of when I became aware of my heart problem, and she said she wasn't sure; she never actually told me I had a heart problem. It was just dealt with in the way that this is what you have to do for now and this is what you have to deal with right now. No overarching discussion was ever had.

My first clear memory is the first traumatic event of my life. I was eight. It was time for the pulmonary valve to be repaired with a more permanent solution than the shunts that were used in early life. I had to have a cardiac catheterization and spent the night in hospital before the procedure. After my parents had gone home for the night, a female doctor came to see me. I remember she told me she would be assisting with the operation the next day and would show me where it was going to be done. I remember her and I remember walking down an empty corridor with her—just the two of us, but nothing more. Apparently, the next morning when my parents arrived at the hospital, I was very upset, although I don't remember it. What I do remember is the procedure, very clearly.

I remember lying on the cold metal operating table. I was completely naked, and I just had some sort of sheets draped across my body and legs, leaving my genital region exposed so they could get to my groins. Above me was a large round light that generated a lot of heat and could be moved up and down. It was positioned low above the table so I could feel the heat coming from it, and I felt constricted with the closeness of it. My wrists were tied to the sides of the bed, or rather slab, below the top edges and with the bright light above me the room seemed rather dark. A cannula was put into my arm at some point for sleeping drugs to be administered.

I could hear my cardiologist somewhere behind me, but it was the female doctor from the night before who stood beside the operating table doing the procedure. I was told that I would feel sleepy, and it would be ok if I drifted in and out of sleep. I remember being nervous, but ok with what was happening, as an eight-year-old I trusted the doctors.

Unfortunately, I never felt the effect of the anesthesia. I never drifted off. Never felt sleepy. I could hear voices around me, see the doctor beside me and occasionally a nurse. The constant heat and hum of the big round light above me seemed to make the experience worse.

Even though my groin areas were slightly numb, I could feel pain and discomfort, that was as far as the anesthetic went. I knew it was important to lie still, but my growing anxiety was becoming hard to ignore. I remember wondering why I hadn't fallen asleep. I whimpered and said it hurt. I said this several times. My cardiologist told me to lie still, which I was doing. The female doctor stopped and looked at me, trying to be comforting I guess, and said something like, 'It'll be over soon, lie still and stop wriggling.'

They didn't believe me. I was wide awake, and it hurt.

◆

In May 2002, Mother's Day, when I was 23 years old, I passed out at the train station. I began to feel dizzy and held onto the railing at the top of the stairs. As I came around, I had the strangest feeling that I was lying on my back in bed, my head turned to the left, the doona pulled up to my chin, with someone moving my left foot from side to side.

'Why is someone moving my foot? I want to sleep,' I thought. I opened my eyes and was no longer in my bed; I never had been. I was lying flat on the walkway at the top of the stairs at Lindfield. A couple were leaning over me, the woman moving my foot. Once I was conscious, they turned me to the side and placed me in the recovery position. The couple called my parents, who arrived shortly before the ambulance. This was the incident that led to the fitting of my first defibrillator, the St Jude. Also known as my heart box.

My heart box is a device to shock my heart back into normal rhythm when it beats too fast, or to pace it to normal rhythm when it beats too slow. The heart box is attached to the heart by wire leads that sense the heart's rhythm. It is like a small computer, containing information about what it needs to do when it senses certain things happening. It also has a long-life battery. My first device had a battery life of about six years. Now I am on my fifth device, a Boston Scientific, the battery is supposed to last ten and a half years. The more the device delivers shocks, the shorter the battery life will be. Shocking requires more energy than pacing. The length of time required to deliver a shock also affects the battery life. It all depends on how much the device is used.

The heart box is small, only weighing a few hundred grams, with two wires or leads attached to it. It is almost square, but the corners are rounded. I have only seen one once. Through the skin, you can see the edge of the box very visibly—it sticks out as it doesn't sit flush with the skin. When I lose weight, it becomes more noticeable, pinching as it resettles in position. As I gain weight it also pinches, but will become less noticeable, although the top inner corner will always stick out because of the angle it sits at. Box Five is much better. It has been placed behind the muscle and so you can't tell it's there. Though when you touch the area, the top inner corner is still more prominent than the rest to look at, all that can been seen now is the surgical scar.

When a new box is put in, it pinches on and off while it settles in its place, which takes about six months each time. As I said, it pinches when I gain or lose weight, but it also pinches when I reach across my body to the left. It pinches when I settle in bed, snuggling under the covers with my hands up under my chin or under the pillow. Pretty much any movement that changes the position of the heart box will make it pinch. I have trained myself not to put my hands under my chin to go to sleep. All this discomfort was very noticeable with the first four heart boxes. Now that number five is behind the muscle, it has been very different. It still took six months to settle, but the almost constant pinching doesn't occur. The pinching when I stretch my arm in a certain way, or lift heavy objects has not been there, and settling in my bed at night is also much more comfortable. I also can't feel it under the skin anymore, meaning I have forgotten it is there. I barely feel it now.

◆

The day before the first heart box implantation surgery I was sitting on my bed, Dad was in the chair beside me reading the ICD—Implantable Cardioverter Defibrillator—booklet. He chuckled and proceeded to read a passage aloud. I didn't look at him, I remember I felt numb, not wanting to be there anymore. The paragraph was about having sex with an ICD and that it may fire during sexual intercourse. He chuckled again and I burst into tears.

Dad stood up and gave me a sideways hug and said it'll be alright. He meant well, but often didn't think before he spoke. I was already 22, how was I going to be intimate with a guy now? It was already going to be difficult to find someone willing to commit to a relationship with me, with all my heart and health problems, now I had to tell a potential boyfriend that if we ever were intimate, there was a possibility that I could have an arrhythmia, and if I received a shock from the device, he would feel it too.

I felt sick. For the first time I really felt like my life was not going to be like everyone else's. I was different and I hated it.

The following day I had the ICD put in, on the wrong side, because they said there was not enough room on the left. When I left hospital, I was given a long list of all the things I could use safely such as microwaves, kettles, stereos, and all the things I had to stay certain distances from such as hair dryers, induction stoves, handheld metal detectors, and what to strictly avoid such as magnets, airport scanners and wands. Retail store sensors were alright if I walked straight through them, but if I stopped they would interfere with the heart box's sensors and if a shock was required, it possibly wouldn't be delivered. I was given strict instructions not to remove the waterproof dressing for two weeks, not to get it wet, and not to lift my arm above the shoulder. It was hard to lift it anyway due to the swelling and soreness.

Simple, daily tasks became difficult. I needed assistance getting dressed and undressed, and getting in and out of the bath, so I didn't put weight on my right arm, my mum also had to wash my hair. I was having to eat, brush my teeth and hair with my left hand, which was unnatural because I'm right-handed.

I felt repulsed. It looked horrible, like an alien trying to escape the confines of my skin. The entire shape of the box could be seen, and the top ridge stuck out further than the bottom. If I ran a finger across the top, I could feel the hard edge. Before this surgery, I only had the two scars on my back running around the shoulder blades, the scar down the centre of my chest and the three drainage scars below that. If you cut me in half, I was symmetrical. I didn't mind people seeing them, although sometimes I was self-conscious and preferred to keep my back covered, it was nothing like how I felt at that moment.

I felt like I resembled a road map, and I wanted to rip the device out.

◆

It takes nine seconds to receive a shock from my ICD. During that time the device needs to analyze what's going on with my heart rhythm, whether it's going to correct itself or not, and charge up enough to deliver the shock. I have experienced arrythmias that have stopped on their own. Those nine seconds can feel like a lifetime, waiting to receive the shock. If I am standing at the time, I quickly find a post or something to hold onto. My vision blurs and I will feel light-headed, as if I am going to faint. Generally, for the next few hours I will feel a bit spaced out, but this doesn't last too long. I had two very memorable episodes of arrhythmia while I was living in England, studying for six months at Sunderland University in 2005.

I was walking from the metro to my student accommodation one evening. It was daylight saving but almost dark. I was crossing the road at the pedestrian lights when I felt the fast heart rate. I was almost across the road and quickly stepped onto the footpath and held onto the metal pole with the button to signal you wanted to cross. I remember it was yellow, rectangular and large, not like in Australia. Holding onto the pole with my right arm, I hugged it a little, but leant a little to the left so I wasn't leaning right up against the traffic light box. I knew that the shock would make me jerk a little so I guess, instinctively I was trying to protect myself by leaning away from it as much as I could.

As with every time I have an arrhythmia, I thought to myself, *come on*. The device fired and I jerked forward. My vision returned to normal, and I straightened up to get my bearings. I took a step away from the pole and as I did so, the pedestrian beeps sounded, even though the one thing I hadn't done was press the button again. I glanced across the road and noticed one car waiting patiently at the traffic lights, but there was no one else around to have pressed the button. I realised that the force of my defibrillator firing had triggered the lights to change. I purposefully walked away from the road, not looking at the car. If only I could have that kind of power whenever I wanted.

The second incident was two days before I flew back to Australia. My friend and I were returning from a holiday in Prague. We flew back into Newcastle airport and were the last off the plane, walking down the steps and following everyone else into the airport building. I was following my friend and then felt my heart going really fast. I dropped to the floor and waited. My friend dropped down in front of me, I'm sure she could see the pain or panic on my face. As I waited for the defibrillator to shock me, I sensed this arrhythmia was different. My eyes weren't blurring, and my heart was pounding the fastest I had ever felt before. This one was definitely more intense. The device shocked me, and I felt like I was out of breath. Two men happened to be walking along the corridor and stopped next to us. I looked in their direction, and said, 'I need a wheelchair'. I knew I wasn't going to be able to walk through the airport. One of them disappeared while the other asked my friend what had happened. She said 'she has a defibrillator.' The man returned with the wheelchair, and they helped me up off my all fours and into it. My friend carried my bag for me. They took us through customs and out to the waiting area to meet my friend's mother and brother who were collecting us. When I saw her mum standing there I burst into tears. I think the emotion of seeing a maternal figure hit me. My friend explained to them what had happened. While she was explaining, the defibrillator fired again. It had never gone off twice before, and that scared me. They asked if I wanted to go to the hospital. I didn't really want to, but I was worried about being ok to fly home. I was given the OK, as well as a letter to take to my routine defibrillator appointment scheduled for when I got back to Sydney.

Back in Australia after my flight I was at Royal Prince Alfred Hospital, I explained what had happened at the airport. The technician was able to view all the episodes of arrhythmias and pacing I had experienced since my previous visit. They explained what had happened was the first shock stopped the fast heartbeat, but the two parts of my heart had started to beat at different speeds, so that is why I received the second shock, to get it back into normal rhythm. I told them it was the worst experience of arrhythmia I had ever had. They said my heart rate went up to 270 beats per minute, where my heart normally sits at about 150 beats per minute—the box will deliver treatment once the heartbeat reaches 170 beats per minute. The attending cardiologist added that I'd experienced eight arrhythmias, four of which required shocks and four hadn't. He said that is not good and I should see Professor Goldberg as soon as possible, who informed me I would need to be put on medication.

While I reluctantly accepted that I didn't really have a choice, I hated the idea of being on medication for the rest of my life, especially because I was so young, and the whole point in choosing the defibrillator in the first place was so I wouldn't have to take medication, now only three years later, I was starting medication anyway and I have a metal box in my chest that I never wanted.

◆

When you are born with a medical condition and you have many medical appointments and hospital stays, surgeries, minor procedures and even a life-threatening infection, it can often seem as if you have constantly suffered, and it can become difficult to pinpoint which was the worst experience or moment.

That said, in 2012, I believe I experienced my worst moment. I was about to undergo a dangerous operation, to remove a wire lead from inside my heart. I had always been told this would never be done because the risk of damaging the heart was too great. Now I was being told there was no other option. I was facing a surgery that was likely life threatening. At a routine defibrillator check-up, a problem was found with one of the leads, but they weren't sure what the problem was. The readings were a bit off, but everything was working fine. I had to go back a month later. The results were the same. It was suggested that I go into the Mater Hospital for an interrogation of the device under anaesthetic. I really fought against it. I felt that they were making things up. I felt fine, so why was I being treated like a machine? The old conflict returned, why was I having to endure so much for a piece of technology that wasn't doing anything anyway now that the medication was working so well?

I was in tears, angry, hurt and I felt betrayed. Reluctantly I agreed to undergo the device interrogation. The results were not good. There was an issue with one of the leads and because I was so small, there was not enough room to slide a new one in. The lead would have to be extracted. I knew from the outset when making the decision to have the ICD back in 2002, that the leads could never be removed because the danger was too great. I reiterated this to Dr Slater. He agreed that was usually the case, but in certain circumstances it could be done. There was only one surgeon specialised enough to perform this surgery and he was at The Prince of Wales hospital.

I was under no illusion that this surgery could kill me. I had lived with that knowledge for years. Now it was real. I made sure my Will was up to date. I made sure my financial papers were all filed. I made sure my passwords were hidden with names of people to contact to ask for help. I made sure this was easily accessible and Mum knew where to find it. I called my friends to say goodbye. The worst was calling my brother and sister just before I went into the surgery to tell them I loved them and to say goodbye; then hugging my Mum and Dad and saying I loved them and saying goodbye.

I believed I would not survive this surgery.

◆

I woke suddenly. I was sweaty. There was an oxygen mask over my mouth and nose, wires all over me, blood pressure cuff on my right arm, and I was surrounded by people.

'I want Mum and Dad,' I had said and was looking around for them. A nurse said I was ok and they were right here. They covered me up with the bed covers, right up to my chin, and removed the oxygen mask. It felt like I was in a coffin. The staff moved away, and Mum and Dad came to stand next to the bed.

'Did it work?' I asked.

'Yes, it worked, it went fine,' Mum answered.

After that they left. The covers were quickly removed, and the staff continued doing whatever they were doing as I fell asleep. I drifted in and out of sleep for the next few hours, but I was aware they had moved me to a ward. When I had first woken up, I thought 'thank God I'm alive' and when Mum answered my question and Dad had patted my shoulder reassuringly, I knew I would be ok. The potentially fatal surgery had worked, and I could get on with my life.

At the age of 33, you do not expect to be faced with a situation like this. To prepare yourself for death. To say goodbye. To have everything in order. My worst experience since having the defibrillator put in, and my best experience happened on the same day.

◆

Now at the age of 45 I look back on my life living with CHD and the heart box, or boxes, and I am filled with a mixture of strength and amazement that I have managed to endure and get through everything I have experienced medically. I am also filled with sadness at knowing what I have missed out on because of having these conditions. The freedom to run, to walk fast without becoming puffed out, being part of a loving relationship and having children and to be treated as an equal, are things I see around me in others every day and yet elude me. Yes, I know I am different, but I still deserve to be an equal and experience the same things as everyone else.

Penny Macoun is a writer from Sydney. Her dream of becoming an author became reality in 2020 when she self-published the first of four picture books: *Gorkle* (2020), *Rollo's Wet Surprise* (2021), *The Christmas Door* (2022) and *Two Can Be Trouble* (2024). Penny was born with her illness and disabilities, but she has never let them stop her doing the things she loves.

This World is Swiftly Passing

Michael Ramsden

'You'll be dead in two years.'

The diagnosis is delivered with clinical detachment. No ambiguity. Any prospect of hope coldly crushed by a monotone voice in a plain brown tie. My stepmother Pamela remembers staring at that brown tie, unaware that tears were falling in rivers. Dad was stoically silent, she said. She calculated. It was October 1999. They had until October 2001, assuming Brown Tie was correct. He was close. Dad died in the early hours of September 20th, 2001. In his final days he could move only one finger.

I'm nearly fifty-six now. My kids are at university, dreaming of futures that seem open-ended and full of possibility. Dad was fifty-six when he was told 'you'll be dead in two years.'

Amyotrophic Lateral Sclerosis (ALS), a form of Motor Neurone Disease (MND), is rare. The disease affects two per 100,000 and there is no single diagnostic test. The need to exclude other neurological conditions results in a tortuous process that can last for months. Lupus. MS. Parkinson's. A lonely dark tunnel where the light recedes with each step, but you focus on that pinprick, desperately hoping for any option that isn't ALS. In the twenty odd years since Dad's diagnosis, the prognosis hasn't changed. More likely in men. No cure. Life expectancy two to five years.

Like his father before him, my father Professor Vic Ramsden was an engineer with a passion for his work. As deputy head of school at the University of Technology, Sydney, he was at the top of his game. In 1999, just before his diagnosis he founded the Centre for Electric Machines and Power Electronics. Jian Guo (Joe) Zhu, former PhD student and now professor himself at the University of Sydney, cheerfully related tales of working with Vic in the lab until midnight. Another colleague, Dr Peter Watterson, marvelled at Dad's work ethic, the way he worked faster than everyone else or would complete complex calculations for grant applications in the early hours of the morning to meet deadlines.

Vic worked almost to the end. In 2001, he published a paper with Peter, Joe and a team of engineers on the application of permanent magnets in electric motor design. I remember seeing pictures of their electric solar car, the Aurora. A beautifully sleek silver and glass butterfly on wheels. My father was a world expert in this rapidly evolving field.

Before his final test results came back, Dad flew to Darwin to speak at a conference. He had recently been to Louisiana, meeting up with his sister Pam and her husband Scott. He joked about the 'two Pamela's' in his life. Later, Pam told me that she'd had an awful feeling of dread. Vic wouldn't say, but he was dragging his foot in this weird way as he walked. On his return from Darwin, Dad and Pamela went back to the hospital to discuss the latest test results. They listened quietly while the details were patiently explained. Asked questions. Reached for slivers of hope.

Yes, you'll be in a wheelchair, but we can cope with that. Stephen Hawking has this disease. He's still alive, Pamela smiled through her tears.

Brown Tie interrupted.

No, you don't understand. Yours is the worst form. You'll be dead in two years.

◆

on the shore

Of the wide world I stand alone, and think
Till love and fame to nothingness do sink.
John Keats

Soft morning light seeps across leathery floorboards. Dust motes dance and sparkle. A breathing machine gently pulses, obediently pressing life into nothingness. Beneath the mask your body lies inert. Wasted.

◆

Memories strobe like a zoetrope reel. A fragment from childhood. Dad sweeps across the lawn pushing his navy blue Flymo. Whirring and buzzing it floats like a mini hovercraft. I watch, transfixed. A twenty-metre yellow cord trails behind. Without warning the mower stops. He's run over the cord. Again. Cursing, he stomps to the garage to splice and fix the cord. Again.

The garage is stacked with reclaimed timber, fence palings and assorted miscellany rescued from adventures to the tip. On the way back we often had more than we started. My brother and I would leap out of our faded green HR Holden Wagon, dart around and climb on top of the rubbish. Dad would find some old electrical cord, an appliance or two and toss it in the car. Something else to fix or else strip for useful parts. And more wood. Always more wood. I thought the tip was magical. An Aladdin's cave of unclaimed treasures.

◆

I wake early and jump into bed with you and Mum. In the middle, the Sunday papers. Arguments over comics and puzzles. You're reading a book. *Poor Fellow My Country*. My child's eye marvels at the scale. Hardback. Mountainous. Images of outback plains and endless sky on the cover. You must have a mind big enough to handle this book.

Every morning you polished your brown lace up shoes. Rhythmically massaging the leather in a precise set of patterns. Sides, heel, sides then finishing with a few swishes across the toe. I'd watch you stride up the road to catch the train, battered leather satchel under your arm. At home, you had the gardening boots. Black and weathered, never polished, scuffed and faded.

◆

How cruel that the disease started with your feet. Your feet fascinated childhood me. Those heels cracked and calloused from years of walking barefoot. I discovered you went to the opera barefoot, and your mother was horrified. She insisted you stay in your seat. You leapt up at interval and mischievously headed off to examine the orchestra pit. Much later you drove to work in the city barefoot, pausing in the carpark to put on shoes, no socks. You rebelled against the need to conform. My father, the scruffy romantic. Walking was your thing. You walked everywhere. Usually striding ahead, making others run to keep up. In 1966 you walked across the globe in a typically adventurous journey crafting stories as you went.

You bushwalked barefoot. You slept on the ground in our tent. No mattress. No floor. You stepped in dog shit so often we nicknamed you 'poo foot'. You hated shoes but eventually the nurse convinced you. Crisp white joggers from The Athlete's Foot. You were angry, aggressive towards an innocent salesperson. Those shoes made you see the truth.

◆

Dad learnt to surf in his early fifties, cherishing his new 'Midget Farrelly' surfboard. He would wake early, head to Avalon for a surf before catching the bus into work. We would watch him wobble off, his wiry wet-suited frame, arms ungainly and long, like a giant spider. He loved telling the story of the day he sliced his leg open in a brutal fin chop, driving himself to hospital holding the flap of skin down. 'Shark bite' he would boast, pointing at his scar with that cheeky grin. Then sometime in early 1999 he began having trouble standing on the board. He switched to kneeling, thinking it was probably a back issue. Then he struggled to walk along the beach, often tripping and stumbling. Next came 'Foot Drop'. Crossing the road, he looked like a gigantic wading bird lifting his right foot in a ludicrous dance. Something was wrong. Very wrong.

◆

You shuffle down the beach, sculpting a snail trail across the sand. Zinc painted kids laugh and careen around in the summer glare. A soft north easterly breeze drifts past. Lifeguards scan the confetti of bobbing heads. Beer cans and barbecues fizz. You smile and wave, masking any discomfort. We called your new way of getting around 'bumming'. You rock forward and dig your hands into the sand, pushing and pulling, like a tortoise instinctively shovelling itself to safety. You splash through the white water and lean back under a wave. Eventually you float. Free like driftwood. Today you're feeling a little stronger. The walking frame sits beside me.

◆

My wife, Julie, and I meet Joe Zhu on a warm summer morning at a café on the grounds of Sydney University. I can see why Dad loved these places. Signs direct you to the 'Immersive Learning Laboratory' and the 'Centre for Sustainable Energy Development'. I remember as a child spending time with Dad at work in the school holidays. Catching the red rattler train from Denistone to the city before walking down the Devonshire Street tunnel to the University of Technology tower building. My brother and I would be left to roam, playing table tennis in the union lounge, catching lifts, and running up and down the stairs. Dad never seemed to worry about where we were.

Unsure if I have the right place, I send Joe a short text. Moments later a jolly Asian man bounces along the path, smiling broadly. His eyes crinkle when he laughs. Like most people I speak to about Dad, he is excited to chat about the person they remember. We order coffee and talk over bubbly laughter from a nearby group of students. Joe reminds me of Dad. There's a sense of youthful energy that seems to rise especially when the conversation turns to work, projects and research. Gently I steer him back to what it was like working with Dad. I wanted to know more about who he was and the experiences they shared. I asked Joe about a story Pamela told me, how Dad took him surfing when he first arrived in Australia from China. 'Oh yes', he said, laughing at the memory, 'I thought I was going to die.' Apparently, Dad had gone off for a surf leaving Joe to swim alone. Avalon is a notoriously dangerous beach with strong rips, and he needed rescuing by a local surf lifesaver. Julie is horrified but Joe and I smile.

The conversation turns to trips they shared together. On a visit to China, Joe related, 'Vic would never eat at a conference, so we always went to the local restaurants. He would try anything on the menu.' Joe and Vic became very close, sharing a passion for their work and an enthusiasm for life. Together they published over twenty papers. Joe cheerfully told me, 'I think Vic and I got on well because I would happily drink with him'. Once in Brisbane they stayed at the conference hotel until closing, using up drink vouchers given to delegates. Joe was exhausted but Vic insisted on finding another bar. They walked everywhere, eventually finding one still open. 'He was so generous, buying drinks until two.' Here Joe pauses briefly, lost in the memory. 'I was so tired, but Vic just kept on going.' In a touching eulogy for UTS News entitled 'a loveable bloke', Peter Watterson wrote, 'he would often be the last one up shouting drinks at the bar'.

Peter is another colleague eager to share stories about Dad. I remember first meeting Peter at a dress up party Dad organised. The theme was LY, for leap year. Peter came as the 'Loy Yang Power Station', wearing an absurd hat with white cotton stuffing pouring out the top. He talked fast and never seemed to stand still. Pamela commented on how different Peter and Joe were, 'but your father loved them both.' During our two-hour phone call, Peter charged through story after story, barely drawing breath. Luckily, I recorded the conversation. Like Joe, Peter had a surfing story. 'We were in Perth on our way back to the hotel. It was a boiling hot day. Driving past Cottesloe Beach Vic suddenly stopped, telling me he was going for a swim. He just jumped out, threw off his clothes and ran into the water!' Once again, this rings true with my memories of Dad, the spontaneous boy scout. 'It wasn't like the water was calm,' Peter added. 'It was really quite rough. I couldn't believe I was watching this naked guy with a bushy beard body surfing in massive waves.' Even Pamela is astonished when I tell her the story, 'Oh Victor … ' she said softly, 'he was just so very alive.'

I speak to Jim Minchin, an old college friend. Dad and Jim received scholarships to Trinity College at Melbourne University, discovering they shared a love of jazz and poetry. Jim said that Dad looked after him. 'I didn't really fit in but your Dad,' he said, 'seemed to be able to get along with everyone.' I also discover Dad was dux of Melbourne Grammar, a fact he never told me. Pam told me of Vic taking her to a Louis Armstrong concert, when she was still just young. Pamela tells me how much Dad loved the poet Tagore. I learn from her that dad fought for years to have poetry included as a compulsory subject for his engineering students. The world didn't need more illiterate engineers, he said.

◆

Dad was a paradox. An engineer who loved to be spontaneous and hated planning ahead. This proved a difficult combination when dealing with the reality of MND. Pamela simply had to force Dad to face each stage. For carers, after the initial shock of diagnosis the emotional weight they bear is compounded by the astonishing speed of progression and rapid pace of decline. Caring becomes an 'all in' hamster wheel of sleepless, crushing, exhausting round-the-clock support. No sooner do you adjust to one stage than the next is upon you in an unstoppable avalanche of progressively more debilitating symptoms. Splints. Walking sticks. Walker. Constipation. Enema. Nurse. Phone calls. Appointments. Bathroom modifications. Vehicle modifications. Single beds. Hospital beds. Feeding decisions. Communication aids. Manual wheelchair. Motorised wheelchair. Hoist. Breathing machine.

While he may have heard Brown Tie's death sentence, Dad never accepted it. He insisted on walking unaided, tripping so often it became a joke. Dylan Thomas exhorted us to, 'rage, rage against the dying of the light' and Dad certainly raged while his body continued towards a terrifyingly inevitable shutdown. Thanks to Pamela's selfless commitment, while the disease ruthlessly froze his body section by section, Dad bought a vintage two-seater sports car, drove to Melbourne (against medical advice), bought a campervan, travelled north, south and west and bought a property in Nimbin. With the wisdom of hindsight, Pamela and I have discussed these decisions many times and the 'madness of it all'. She herself was suffering from cardiomyopathy and her specialists bluntly told her she would not cope. She wrote in her diary at the time, 'Well, I'll just have to'.

We sip our cups of tea, sigh and agree this frenzied activity represented Dad's passion for life and a characteristically stubborn determination to write his own story in defiance of those who would say no. Psychologists have noted we create these stories to make order of disorder. This 'drive to story' seems particularly strong when confronted with death, loss, and grief. At the monthly multi-disciplinary team meetings where his condition was discussed, Dad happily let student interns interview him and poke at his body. Each time the room of specialists began their assessment with; 'so tell us, what crazy adventures have you been on now'?

In the midst of this Julie and I were going through our own experience of testing and specialist visits. We had been trying for our first child with no success, even reaching that stage where you accept that perhaps you just won't have kids. Then in April we discovered Julie was pregnant. The baby was due in December 2001. I wanted to be alone with Dad when I told him. 'That's good news,' he said quietly. I remember his eyes. Those blue pools drifted away as a thin film of mist formed and we didn't speak.

◆

Nimbin was a connection to the sublime. The name comes from the Nimbinjee spirit people protecting the area and its surrounding ranges are rich with stories reaching back to the Dreamtime. It is known as a place of healing. The property address was 1024 Mountain Top Road. Twenty acres resting under soaring granite towers, the Nimbin rocks. It was his escapist Xanadu from a world of pain and confusion.

Dad made the decision to buy the property after being told he would need to make plans, due to Pamela's condition, for intensive nursing care. Faced with a world that was rapidly closing around him, he convinced Pamela to ignore the specialist's concerns. Fortunately, they found a supportive local community and exceptional palliative care. Studies have identified four consistent storylines in patient responses to a diagnosis of MND: sustaining, enduring, preserving and fracturing. I'm not surprised to learn that Dad slips neatly into the fracturing storyline. In this scenario researchers describe a patient for whom the abandonment of personal and professional plans is shattering. They choose to live in denial of reality, in a surreal notion of time.

I'm curious about this stage of Dad's illness and manage to track down Alan, his carer in Nimbin. Now living in Perth and still working in palliative care, Alan echoes the enthusiastic delight I have become used to when the subject of Dad comes up. I remember Alan as wiry, gay and incredibly caring. Pamela liked him instantly and after Dad's passing, offered him free use of a cottage on their property.

'Your Dad taught me a lot,' Alan tells me in another lengthy conversation. 'He was my first MND patient. I still use him as inspiration for other MND sufferers.'

I'm curious about what made Dad so unique in Alan's eyes.

'He always had things to do. He never let the disease define him. We would laugh all the time, especially when it was time for the enema. I had to massage his perineum and he'd joke about how good it felt. He wasn't self-conscious about his body.'

Dad calmly told Joe about his diagnosis over lunch, patiently explaining the stages he would go through. Joe was shocked that Vic seemed so calm. He offered to help him with Chinese remedies, but Vic wouldn't accept anything like that. They were not logical in his opinion. He was so stubborn.

◆

I pull down the heavy steel ramp, bolted to the floor of the campervan. We're heading into Lismore to look for a new television. It's mid-afternoon and you decided we had to go. There and then. You line up the wheelchair, push the stubby joystick forward and roll into the back, head rocking and nodding. I had to drive carefully; every corner was painful. The disease makes your skin hypersensitive. We park at the back of the store, where there is a ramp. I start to look at screens on the wall. Then I notice you staring at the enormous rear projection model sitting in the middle of the floor. You want that don't you. You giggle mischievously. I understand. This monumental grey sculpture is absurd, impractical, an illogical extravagance for a man who argues about spending money on basic home repairs. Yes, we can deliver but not until next week. Sorry, I need it now. OK but this is the floor model, we'll have to find the box. Then find the box, I'll park in the loading dock. We're taking it today.

Somehow, we squeezed you in first then slid that heavy box behind. Once upon a time we bought a giant TV.

◆

Looking back, in order to live his life 'out of time', I think Dad was constantly inventing, continuing to solve problems and teach others. For over twenty years he voluntarily designed and built technical aids to enrich the lives of those whose worlds had been shrunk by society's inadequate provision for people with a disability.

'It was just so, so cruel,' Pamela tells me, 'He worked on the motor for that breathing machine he had to use.'

I also discover in a conversation with George Winston, founder of Technical Aid to the Disabled, that Dad's first invention was a communication device for a patient with 'locked in syndrome'. In the mid 1970's, Dad built a machine that consisted of a set of lights which cycled through the alphabet, stopping when the patient blinked. For many years Dad taught rehabilitation engineering at UTS, working with students on pioneering aids including an eye operated keyboard. His passion for social justice reflected in the hours spent on these aids.

Faced with his own world rapidly shrinking, Dad created spaces where he could still be project manager, philosopher, critic, lover and adventurous larrikin. He maintained his sense of identity, taking decisions that enabled him to keep on living in the face of constant change. In death, subjects become objects, people become things. Dad refused to become an object, another patient to be managed by a medical model that dictated his final months and weeks should be 'comfortable'. Instead as the disease crippled him and his breathing became more laboured, he created new stories in a furious rebellion against time and truth. He ordered more furniture from Aldo, discussed home renovations with Pixie and teased Alan about his taste in shirts. Before he died, he wanted to live.

◆

The breathing mask that bruises your face. The hoist to help you out of bed. The feeding tube to pump you full of Sustagen.

I watch while you have your feet massaged. They are swollen, like small watermelons, grotesque representations of your condition. You can't move your feet. Your legs appear from under a cotton sarong, silently wasting away. Ingrid, the German masseur, gently lifts each foot, rubbing tenderly. She visits every day, part of the parade of Nimbin locals who joined your story. Aldo the furniture maker, Pixie the builder, John the handyman. You loved to engage them all in conversation. Thankfully your voice lasted almost until the end.

Afternoon sun bathes the room in gentle light. A small ray catches your head, permanently slumped to one side. The shadow on the floor becomes a distinct silhouette, traced out behind the wheelchair. You can't hold your head straight, your neck muscles have faded, but you smile at Ingrid and your eyes wrinkle. We used to joke about organising intimate massages by busty Swedish models. There's jazz music playing and fresh mangoes in the fruit bowl. A plastic cup with a long drinking straw sits close by. Your fingers can't grip so you hold the cup using your hands like tongs. Ingrid finishes and rolls on the white compression socks. Now your feet look like bloated silkworms, cocooned in their sacks.

◆

You're wearing your usual blue sarong, much easier to manage than trousers and more dignified than a hospital gown. I don't want to do this. Usually, the nurse or Pamela assisted you, but this morning it's just us. Morning rain drifts in misty waves. Your sapphire blue eyes look into me as I pull up a chair and put the clear bottle to one side, its spout angled up like a healthy pitcher plant. My hands feel mechanical, disconnected. I pause briefly and you smile softly before nodding encouragement. I take a breath of humid, sticky air and gently lift the folds of soft cotton, taking care to avoid touching you until I am completely ready. It's resting limply on a bed of tight curls. I haven't seen you naked and this close since childhood. I often watched you swim, those distinctively languid strokes as you glided through the water wearing those faded pink speedo's, your 'bathers'. I remember you in the public showers. Never in a cubicle, always in the open space. Your tall, slender body bare apart from a small tuft of chest hair and a wispy snail trail leading to a dense pubic afro. You often walked around the house naked.

I reach for the bottle and curl my thumb and two fingers around, carefully placing you inside. A weak yellow stream dribbles out. You smile again and I turn away, offering you the smallest degree of privacy.

◆

I'm holding a teardrop shaped vase. It's a beautiful piece of Swedish Orrefors glass bought on impulse from the factory in 1979. An inner sleeve of turquoise, emerald and amber tinged with a lutescent glow floats inside a crystal-clear casing. I have this piece, together with a hardwood table carved from a single tree. Another impulsive purchase from a woodworker's exhibition at the Sydney Opera House. Dad's romantic spirit breathes from these pieces. Death takes away the physical person, leaving memories infused in such objects. I yearn for his company. He recognised the enduring power of art, poetry and music to connect us with the eternal, valuing the imagination and its embodiment in creative passion. Sunlight briefly catches the vase, refracting and dancing. I am grateful for his life and the stories we shared.

◆

A world of silence on fire.
(Tagore)

Michael Ramsden is an English teacher at a public comprehensive high school on the NSW South Coast. A passionate educator, in 2023 he completed his Master of Creative Writing at Macquarie University. Michael has presented at English Teachers' Association conferences and published articles in the association journal. He is the author of several books for younger readers and enjoys reading and writing crime fiction.

The Anatomy of Rage

Jessica Kirkness

On my torso are four pink scars. Two sit on either side of my hip bones, one slightly to the left of my midline, and the other—the most jagged and unsightly—lives in my belly button. In June of last year, these were the sites my surgeon's laparoscope and implements entered my body. For several hours, he scraped around inside of me, and when I woke, my abdomen inflated like an overfull balloon, blood pooled beneath the gauze that covered the incisions. Months on, my bellybutton still resembles the sewing projects I attempted in high school, my flesh puckered at its new seams.

Throughout the summer I kept them hidden, opting for full piece swimming costumes and clothing that kept me covered. As my incisions healed, my pelvis remained as it has been for years—a tyrant demanding my attention: the thing that determined a good or a bad day, being upright or confined to my bed.

My surgery confirmed something I had long suspected. I had endometriosis in tissue behind my uterus, bowel, rectum, and ovaries. After the procedure, my doctor told me that my insides looked 'angry.' He showed me photographs of my affected organs. They were bloodied and inflamed, covered in lesions. 'Stage three,' he said. 'You weren't making it up.' He also determined I had adenomyosis: the lesser-known sister of endo, where the endometrium or lining of the uterus, grows into the uterine walls. The only known, and imperfect 'treatment' for this is hysterectomy. There is no cure.

Endometriosis is a condition that affects one in nine women and people assigned female at birth. It occurs when tissue similar to endometrium begins growing in places it shouldn't. Endo can cause inflammation, digestive issues, extreme pain, and infertility. Many assume that its symptoms last during menstruation alone. But in many cases they occur at random, coming in waves or 'flares' that can last several weeks or more. Once, in the middle of a flare, my mother tried to soothe me over the phone. 'Try and think about a time without pain,' she suggested. 'and go there in your mind. I couldn't recall one, certainly not since childhood, and burst into tears.

While the symptoms vary from person to person, the disease can be debilitating. Levels of pain don't necessarily accord with level of severity either. My surgeon explained to me that he's seen patients at stage one (the least severe) where pain is a constant obstacle, and cases of stage four where the patient is unbothered. Sometimes patients in the latter category receive a diagnosis incidentally or after struggling with fertility. But though it's as common as diabetes or breast cancer, endometriosis is so under-researched and underdiagnosed that most women wait an average of six and a half years for a diagnosis. I waited sixteen.

Initially, having a name to put to my symptoms brought some relief, vindication too. Having been turned away from countless emergency departments, reminded that pain is an expected part of periods, and quizzed by doctors about my mental health—*Could I be anxious? Perhaps imagining things?*—I lay in my recovery bed clutching the images my surgeon had left me. Relief gave way to rage. I was fucking furious.

For the longest time, I had been treated like a recalcitrant child—a girl crying wolf. The vindication was bittersweet. It reminded me of a time my mother sent me to school despite my protests that I was ill. After checking me over, she put me on the school bus where I promptly vomited over the cheap pleather seats 'See?' I'd wanted to say. 'I *told* you so.'

Just two weeks before the operation, I had been sitting in the office of another specialist responsible for treating my other inflammatory pelvic conditions, which are common in endo patients. When I announced my plan to have surgery, she told me it was, 'A waste of time and resources.' According to her, women with endometriosis don't tend to faint with pelvic pain; something I had been doing since I was sixteen. I cited the example of my mother, who had endometriosis all her life and repeatedly fainted on the first day of her period. The doctor shrugged her shoulders and suggested I should cancel.

◆

My experience with the medical system has been maddening; a series of disappointments so endless that revisiting them makes me bristle. The process of coming to a diagnosis often felt like being trapped in a washing machine. So relentless was the cycle—of doctor after doctor, dead end after dead end—that the journey had the flavour of being caught in loops.

When I first reported symptoms to a GP, I was put on the pill—a common first line intervention for 'women's issues'. For a time, this seemed to work. My periods were lighter, and I was spared the horror of previous episodes which left me passed out on the bathroom floor. The pain was excruciating. On every occasion, the spasms were so intense that I'd vomit and have diarrhoea at once. The pill was a godsend but far from failproof. I soon began having breakthrough episodes. When my body resumed its violent outbursts, I was referred to my first specialist.

I was 19 and she believed me straight away; something I took for granted at the time. I'd been subjected to every test possible: abdominal and pelvic ultrasounds, blood tests and internal examinations to rule out any other conditions, but there is currently no way of diagnosing endometriosis outside of surgery. I was scheduled right away.

When my specialist found nothing, we were both shocked. I was sent away with a script for 'Ponstan' and a diagnosis by exclusion: 'dysmenorrhea' or painful periods. I remained on the pill and for a few years the pain was manageable, intermittent. By the time I was 25, I started experiencing a host of new symptoms—weight loss, anaemia, hair loss, and pain during sex.

This time around, I sought a second opinion. I approached a new specialist who puzzled over my symptoms, remarking 'how strange' as I recounted the pain that came on like lightning after sleeping with my partner. I told the doctor that it felt identical to my bad periods; that I broke out in a cold sweat and was overcome by nausea. After examining me, he determined my body was behaving as if I was being 'kicked repeatedly in the balls.' I couldn't help but smirk, imagining how swiftly a doctor might respond to a pair of testicles were they in the room.

This doctor referred me on, unsure what to do with me. In total, I saw five different gynaecologists—enduring the same battery of tests each time—before receiving my diagnosis through surgery.

Beyond gynaecologists, I have spent tens of thousands of dollars on pelvic floor physiotherapy, exercise physiology, and a host of other specialists: urologists, gastroenterologists, immunologists, to determine and treat the cause of my pain. This quest led me to other diagnoses: interstitial cystitis, for example, a condition that affects the bladder and pelvic floor, causing symptoms similar to a urinary tract infection. It's a condition often found in patients with endo, as are the IBS-like symptoms I was experiencing. And yet, even as these other diagnoses racked up in my medical history, it was hard to get anyone to take me seriously.

The worst, most infuriating experiences I've had played out in the emergency departments of Sydney's hospitals. On these occasions, I've turned up doubled over, cradling my insides, desperate for answers. One time I was sent home because it was a Sunday and apparently some major hospitals don't do scans on the sabbath. Another time, when I was passing blood clots the size of fifty cent pieces, bleeding both vaginally and rectally during the middle of my cycle—another tell-tale sign of endo—a young male doctor quizzed me about my sex life and suggested I might have an STI. When I assured him there was little to no chance of this—it was the middle of lockdown, I was single, and hadn't seen a soul in months let alone slept with them—and emphasised the family history of endometriosis, he looked at me sceptically, eyebrows raised, and continued with his line of inquiry. 'Are you sure you haven't had any unprotected sex?' he asked again. 'Positive,' I said.

Regardless, I agreed to a full STI screen. As I lay on the bed, he prepared a speculum and testing kits. As he fumbled about, visibly uncomfortable, he instructed me to remove my underwear. 'Here's a gown to preserve your dignity,' he said without looking me in the eye. I wondered about the dignity of a woman's unclothed body, a body in pain. Until then, I hadn't realised that mine was in question.

When I was discharged without a referral, without a consult from the gynaecological registrar, and without any pain relief, I wanted to scream. The doctor handed me a script for antibiotics in case an infection showed up in the tests. Antibiotics had previously given me terrible bouts of thrush, which aggravated my pain and could last for weeks even with treatment. I told him I'd wait for the results before subjecting myself to that likely outcome. He let out a little scoff and I went home. Three days later, I got a phone call from the hospital. Somehow, there had been a clerical error, and my test results had been lost. Best take some antibiotics anyway, I was told. Within days, I had thrush.

I wanted to march down to the hospital and give somebody, anybody, a piece of my mind. I wanted to rip up my discharge papers—the ones that read 'nil distress' despite my sobbing and writhing in pain—to turn over the carts of supplies and testing kits, and wail. Instead, I swallowed my bile and tossed around in bed, grinding my teeth so hard that I woke the next morning with a pounding headache.

◆

I resented this experience, and countless others like it. On one level, I recognised the doctor was just doing his job; he was trained to identify and eliminate possible causes. He was also working in a system that is chronicly over-stretched and underfunded. He was probably doing his best under less than ideal circumstances of his own. But on another, I knew I was up against an invisible and impenetrable impasse.

I was acutely aware of the 'pain gap' that exists between men and women when receiving healthcare; that while women report it more often, and in more lasting and severe levels than men, they are nonetheless treated for pain less aggressively. Countless studies confirm an implicit bias among physicians, where women are routinely viewed as being histrionic in their complaints. Women are more likely to be given sedatives where men are given pain relief. A 2018 study in the Medical Journal of Australia found that women are half as likely to receive proper heart attack treatment and twice as likely to die six months after a serious heart attack. If you're a woman of colour, implicit bias has been seen in everything from mental health treatments, breast cancer outcomes, and childbirth. Black patients are 40% less likely to receive medication for acute pain compared to white patients.

Despite my privilege as a white, educated, middle-class woman, my emergency doctor decided it more probable that I was a liar—an unreliable narrator both of my pain and my 'promiscuity'—than the likelihood of a legitimate illness.

Endometriosis patients frequently speak of medical gaslighting, where they're told their symptoms are 'all in their head.' Our experiences are all exhaustingly, almost mind-numbingly similar, so much so that I can barely read them without groaning. The overlaps in our stories are so obvious that it can feel costly to bear witness—to absorb yet another account of a woman screaming into the void. Many of us have been dismissed, ignored, treated as if we're hysterical or a hypochondriac. On occasions I've believed myself to be speaking in a calm and measured tone, I've had doctors instruct me to 'take a deep breath,' 'relax,' or my favourite—'chill.'

In isolation, these things might seem small-fry, mildly irritating or clumsy. But the cumulative effect is crushing. Whatever quaint faith I had in the medical system has long disappeared. No matter how my trust has eroded, a cruel fact remains—I need doctors. I continue to be dependent upon their care. There's a good chance my symptoms will recur, as they do for many others. I will probably need repeat surgeries, especially if I plan on having biological children.

For that reason, anger has felt an unproductive, and unpalatable, state to thrash about in. I've dismissed it, buried it, consciously removed the stain of it from my otherwise pleasant demeanour. I know too well that any hint of emotion, will immediately discredit me in the eyes of medical onlookers. As a result, I've developed a clinical matter-of-factness in my appointments. Much in the way I brace myself for the cold sensation of a speculum or ultrasound wand shoved up me, I anticipate, even expect to struggle with my doctors. In order to be believed, I've learned to compose myself, taming my face lest it betray me in my quests for help.

When a colleague read an earlier draft of this essay, she remarked upon my tone, how measured and even-tempered it was. Where was the evidence, the substance of my rage? What I had written was poised, tame. The irony was lost on neither of us and I found myself contemplating the various strategies I've adopted to manage, even straitjacket the feelings that surge beneath the surface.

For example, I developed the habit of 'power dressing' in my appointments. I do this in a rather pathetic bid for status, knowing that my blazers and tailored trousers convey a kind of 'put-togetherness' required of a credible witness at her own trial. It's a habit I picked up at work. I teach undergraduate students at a university in Sydney, and because I'm baby-faced and am often mistaken for a student myself, dressing up has been a helpful point of differentiation; something that prevents me being mistaken for a peer. Clothing, as it is for many women, is my armour. But though it functions as a shield, sometimes as leverage, it doesn't change the game. It's merely an individual play in a broken system.

On other occasions I've inadvertently worked this system. Recently, a new GP at my local practice refused some tests I'd requested, and I found myself calling up again, asking for a follow up. He wasn't available that day, so another doctor took a medical history on his behalf. She took down my profession and asked personal questions, therefore finding out I'd recently completed a PhD. She must have noted this in my file because the next day, the new doctor phoned me back, addressed me with my title, and provided me with the tests and referral I'd asked for. He even enquired about my research. Where he'd previously been breathless and exasperated, my doctor was now curious and concerned.

When we hung up, I wanted to throw my phone across the room. Nothing I'd said had changed his mind. My title had made the difference.

I went for a walk and complained to a friend. As I paced around, fuming, she asked a pressing question: 'What would happen if you complained?' What I heard in my mind—something that excited and panicked me—was 'what would happen if you got *angry*?'

◆

In recent feminist thought, much has been said about reclaiming female anger. During 2018, a flurry of books and articles were written on the topic: Soraya Chemaly's *Rage Becomes Her*, Gemma Hartley's *Fed Up*, Brittney Cooper's *Eloquent Rage* and Rebecca Traister's *Good and Mad* are just a few examples. The collective outpouring of such sentiment led Bitch Media to declare that 'The Future is Furious.' In 2023, Gina Rushton wrote incisively about the 'alchemising power of anger' for those living with endometriosis.

In a similar vein, Lucia Osborne-Crowley's 'Nothing Good Can Come of This' advocates for the healthy expression of anger. Acknowledging the ways that women are socialised into relational peacekeeping, she writes about her struggle to dissociate anger from abuse; the ways the feeling was sublimated and converted to fear and anxiety. For many years, she perceived it as a destructive force, one that would align her with the position of 'abuser' and might turn her into a monster. Instead of expressing anger, she got sad. She cried until she earned sympathy. This reflex, the black and white thinking, she claims, failed to account for the benefits of anger: the boundary setting, the drive for justice, the opportunity for change. 'Anger is a complex emotion,' she writes, 'which is exactly why my child-brain suppresses it, and exactly why we as a society are afraid of it.'

Citing Leslie Jamison's New York Times essay: 'I used to Insist I Didn't Get Angry. Not Anymore,' Osborne-Crowley unpacks Jamison's claim about feeling sadness as a substitute for rage. 'The thing that underlies, 'I don't get angry, I get sad'', she writes, 'is the idea that those who are polite, people-pleasing, responsible, high-achieving and kind and not the *type of people* who get angry. This is, of course, sometimes true. But in some cases, the equation is the wrong way around. The truth is that people *become* polite, people-pleasing, and responsible because they do not feel safe enough to express their anger.'

When I read these reflections, the stifling of my own rage began to make sense. If safety is a precondition for its expression, many others are surely yet to grapple with it. When women feel unsafe on the streets, on public transport, even in their own homes, how are we to tackle anger? And in hospitals and doctor's surgeries where I've scarcely felt safe to be in pain, how could I begin to reckon with it?

For Osborne-Crowley, it was only through working with a therapist that she was able to locate and identify her anger. My own therapist has encouraged me to scan my body in order to identify anger and where it resides within me. These days, I'm better at acknowledging the tension in my jaw, the flicker of strain in my temples, or the tightness in my chest. When I register these sensations, I walk myself back through the day to identify the cause. Though it can feel laborious, sometimes even indulgent, I am undoing the years of feminine comportment—not just the years of prioritising even-temperedness but addressing the voice within who insists that a mad woman is a liability.

As Gabrielle Jackson writes in *Pain and Prejudice*, 'Women are supposed to have pain but suffer in silence, then become invisible after menopause. We aren't supposed to be angry, or demand answers. We are supposed to be nice. Put up with it. Be quiet and supportive of others.' She also points to the many taboos around women's bodies; the myths and legacy of periods being linked to uncleanliness; the ways menstrual blood is still seen as a leakage that transgresses bodily boundaries; the ways our reproductive systems end up foreign to us because of insufficient education around women's health. This and the fact that up until the late 20th century, women were scarcely included in medical trials, meaning that our understanding of biology is largely acquired from studying men.

The silence and stigma around periods accounts for at least some of my trouble navigating my endo journey. When I first got my period at the age of fourteen, I was squeamish. Though I'd attended the mandatory sex education classes in grade six, and had learned about the menstrual cycle, the secret shame of my changing body made me frightened to tell my parents when it arrived. I was so determined to keep it to myself, that I made makeshift sanitary items out of make-up removal pads stuck together with sticky-tape. Eventually, I told my mother. She told my father. I was mortified.

◆

I expected to feel angry when I received my diagnosis. What I didn't expect was the shame that crept in like a shadow. After the first wave of indignation, I found myself gripped by feelings of inadequacy. With confirmation of a condition that threatened my fertility, I began looking over photographs I'd taken of my bloated stomach to show my doctors—endo sufferers refer to this as 'endo-belly'. In some of these images I look several months pregnant. This illusion began to feel especially cruel. I wondered if this was as close as I would come to pregnancy.

For many people with endo, the spectre of pregnancy is both a tender topic and double bind given that doctors have historically recommended it as a solution for pain. In the 1950s and 60s, this advice was based off a handful of case reports of patients who experienced a reduction in their symptoms during pregnancy and breastfeeding. When my mother had three children in rapid succession following surgery, she found enormous relief. But for most women, this is a temporary reprieve, and symptoms tend to recur throughout or immediately afterwards. Pregnancy as a cure for endo has long been classed as myth, but there are medical professionals who continue to encourage it despite the lack of reliable evidence in its favour.

Because endometriosis is an illness that threatens your reproductive status as well as your sex life, I found myself re-assessing—however archaic such a notion—my own womanhood. I began to make crude assessments of my sexual market value. I was single at the time of surgery. How would I disclose my illness to future partners?

Though I was disgusted by these thoughts and their readiness to undo me, I had to confront their power, symbolic and otherwise. The more I sat with the feelings, the more I found myself grappling with an internalised Madonna/whore complex. Despite imagining myself as a crusader against such patriarchal nonsense, both poles of acceptable femininity were suddenly thrown into chaos. I could hardly be a vixen in such pain, and now the function of my uterus was in question. Perhaps I should have rejoiced in the radical potential of throwing both archetypes in the bin, but instead, I was grieving. My internal monologue was as insidious as the illness itself.

The surgeon who diagnosed me suspects that endo was lurking inside me during my first laparoscopy. Some of the lesions he removed were so well-established, he found it hard to believe there was nothing there all those years ago. Endo is sneaky, sometimes hard to find, and can even appear in microscopic form. One 2020 study found that 39% of patients undergoing surgery for pelvic pain with no obvious endometriosis lesions were found to have microscopic endometriosis upon biopsy. As a result of these findings, the researchers recommended peritoneal biopsies for all patients undergoing this surgery.

In March of 2022, $58 million of funding for endometriosis was announced. Under the Federal Government's plan, $17.4 million has now been spent on establishing on 22 specialist endometriosis and pelvic pain clinics across the country, and $25.5 million on access to Medicare-funded MRI scanning. Part of this funding has also been dedicated to education and raising awareness of the condition among doctors and the general community. This is the largest ever investment in endometriosis treatment and research in Australia, and when the announcement flashed across my phone, I exhaled. Finally, weight (and money) was being thrown behind the cause. But my anger remained. I speculated about how the money would address the pain gap in real terms. How would the dismissiveness of doctors be addressed?

I am familiar with pain. I can rate it on my doctor's scale. I can describe it in metaphors: the kind that feels like an electrical current running through my organs, or the type that feels like a hot knife being thrust inside me. Other times it's a low moan, a weight bearing down on my pelvic floor. When my symptoms flare, which they can do at any time even post-surgery, it can feel as though my entire reproductive system might fall out of me like foundations giving way to a flood.

But I am without a language for anger, much less for shame. Even as I write this, I am conscious of the fact that I am outing myself as someone chronically ill. I think about my boss or my students reading this and judging me less able or willing to work. There is risk in exposure, in claiming an identity that conjures up connotations of lack. But there is equal risk in silence.

Social researcher, Brené Brown writes about the value of what she calls 'speaking shame' in treating and understanding its impact on women. Developing a fluency in discussing our most inner shame allows for the feelings to be externalised, thereby leading to strategies that increase resilience. I am speaking mine here in the hope of making space. In relinquishing shame and its punishing silence, perhaps I might arrive at rage and its fiery lexicon.

Jessica Kirkness is the author of *The House With All The Lights On*, a memoir about growing up with two Deaf grandparents. She has a PhD in the fields of Life Writing and Disability Studies, and teaches nonfiction writing at Macquarie University. Her writing has been shortlisted for various prizes such as The Richell Prize for Emerging Writers, The Peter Blazey Fellowship, and the Writing NSW Varuna Fellowship. Jessica's work has been published in *Meanjin, The Guardian, Women's Agenda, The Conversation*, and academic journals.

TRANSPLANTATION

A ROMANCE OF LIVE ORGAN DONATION AND WHITE, UNSETTLED PRIVILEGE

Kim Kelly

transplant—*verb* (*t*)

1. to remove (a plant) from one place and plant it in another.

2. Surgery to transfer, as an organ or a portion of tissue, from one part of the body to another or from one person or animal to another.

3. to remove from one place to another.

4. to bring (a colony, culture, etc.) from one country to another for settlement.

Macquarie Dictionary

◆

Three days before Christmas, I am delirious with triumph, escaping from Westmead Hospital with Deano for the first time post-surgery. My little kidney—plump, and pink as my summer frock—is rushing with new life inside my lanky lover and his eyes are so blue, after almost two years dulled with illness, I swim giddily within them as we board the river ferry at Parramatta, citybound.

Sun tinselling the water all the way to the Quay, we wander across the Botanic Gardens to the Art Gallery, where we laugh at all the gilt-framed epic fantasies there as if we'd never seen them before. And then over the road at the Pavilion Cafe, I don't want coffee. I want to crush gum leaves against my skin like a homecoming Anzac. I want to have sex like we're the only two lovers that ever lived. Bit too soon for that, though.

Shush. We are perfect. We have decided our own narrative and the circumstances by which we have conquered death.

We make our way across town to see the flowers in Martin Place, the giant horseshoe wreath laid around the back of the railway steps, monument to the hostages killed at the nearby Lindt Café by a terrorist the previous Tuesday. My heart falls to pieces for their families, their lovers, all the flowers wilting in the sticky December heat. But still joy surges. Incongruous and unstoppable.

Euphoria. For the successful kidney transplantee—that is, Deano—it's not uncommon for there to be an intense rush of wellness, feelings of liberation, a desire to bellow a great big born-again yahoo. But being a laconic sort, he doesn't want much more than to hold my hand incessantly and have Thai for dinner, since his sense of taste has returned with decent renal function. Taste: it's a marvel in itself. Something else I'll never understand beyond the deep-bone, deep-spirit knowledge that all things are related. Butterfly wings and tidal waves. Loose-balloon strings and sealing wax.

I am off my face, drunk with love and victory. Didn't say anything about that kind of reaction in the living-donor literature. There'd been warnings of altruism gone wrong, of regret and complications, physical and emotional. Of course, I didn't listen to any of that. I was too blinded by the need to stop Deano from dying.

Now he's larger-than-life alive. I can't even remember which of my kidneys was harvested—the left or the right? There was a change of plans at the last minute, literally just before I went under, and while I remember being informed, I really didn't care. Just as I don't care this minute about the bruising in my belly and the twinges in the keyhole cuts. I have been too intent on winning. And I have won.

I am greedy for this life. Beyond the funereal flowers, beyond the cenotaph, the city's plastic tree is twenty-metres high, dotted with gaudy baubles, and I am the pink star glittering on top.

◆

A kidney is shaped like a tree, one bowed over on its side by the force of storms. A tiny but mighty tree of life, veins and arteries branch through its fist-sized canopy of rose-coloured blooms, each pulsing with a multitude of nephrons, thready cells that cleanse the blood.

Without kidneys, our vital systems would shut down, the lights would dim within us, and we'd fade away, a planet overwhelmed by its own poisons. Fortunately, most of us are born with two of these handy filters, but by some quirk of evolutionary generosity we only need one to do the job—which is why most of us, so long as we're otherwise tiptop, can give the extra little kidlet to someone else in need.

When I looked into Deano's kind blue eyes for the first time across a café table in Katoomba in the spring of 2008, I formed an instant attachment to him. Shy, quietly brilliant about rocks and maths, he was my muse de bloke from that moment. It was a random dating-app match, and when we finished our coffee we went for a walk in the woods; he held out his hand and I took it. Extraordinary. I'd never done anything like that before; I'd never felt so sure about anything before, either. And I never imagined we'd be bonded in this way one day, flesh to flesh. My flesh inside his.

Now, on New Year's Day 2015, leaving Westmead for the last time, we're stocked up with anti-rejection medications, ready to get on with life. Real life. Deano calls his kidney-gift Lucy, from the Latin for light, and I smile at the roses in his cheeks, gratitude sweeping us west over the Mountains to Millthorpe: a small town still new to this city-girl.

I have forgotten how, when he was very ill, renal action winding down to around five percent by a cruel mechanism of inherited disease, I would cry in the shower so that he couldn't see or hear my sadness and terror as he got sicker and sicker and thinner and thinner. My prayers to no one: please, I can't lose this love of my life. Lover of *my* life. It took me forty years to find him. I have forgotten how afraid I was that his body would reject this small offering from mine. But it hasn't.

Let the pain and the past fall away and away into the breakdown lanes.

Up a dirt track and around a bend, a eucalypt towers behind our house: a gift, as yet unwrapped, under the tree for me. Home. Perhaps. I'm not sure what home is.

◆

Outside my kitchen window, the tree changes with the light, limbs kissed with gold in the dawn, boughs turned to black lace against the sunset. It must be at least twenty metres tall; taller when thunderclouds bloom at its back and it looks as if it might stride across the paddocks, its broad, lower branches whipping out a graziers' warning.

This morning, its leaves are a khaki tracery etched into a blushing, baby-blanket sky, and high, bronze-tipped summer grass glistens all around its feet in worship. I'm not sure what kind of tree it is. A neighbour told me it's a red rivergum, but classification has never seemed relevant to any attempt at describing its singular majesty. Every morning, for the past seven years, it's been the first tree I see as I stand here at the window waiting for the kettle to boil. Less friend than judge, it dominates this land and my first thoughts.

This land is Wiradjuri Country, home to the people of the rivers—the Kalare, Wambuul and Marrambidya—unceded territory, fiercely defended in the Bathurst War of 1824, a conflict that remains unsettled by any treaty. To the northwest, on the peaks of the Canobolas range, men would gather for their sacred ceremonies, and I often wonder if they walked under the branches of this tree on their way southwards to join forces with their general, Windradyne, planning their attack on the rum-soaked British soldiers down in Kings Plains—a ten-minute drive through the green and gold hills from my house. My romantic imagination sees these Wiradjuri warriors emerging from winter mists, possum-skin cloaks shimmering above purposeful strides—and they are completely uninterested in my opinion about anything.

I am remembering.

Deano and I bought this place when he was dying and we were waiting for our transplant date. With mortality so close I could feel its breath upon my ear, I began scrabbling through stories and breadcrumb trails of all kinds searching for truths. Where was I, really? Who was I, really? The worried glances from friends and family underscored all my questions. 'You're moving where?' they'd ask, and I'd pluck up a cheery grin. Yep, me and all my metropolitan sensibilities and myriad anxieties were off to a small patch of nowhere on a lonely ridgetop, snow-dusted in June and oven-fried in January, where my writing life would flourish in the face of doom and a dodgy internet connection.

It was early, wattle-burnished September when I began unpacking, and I was silently scared of everything. That my kidney wouldn't be good enough; I wasn't good enough to do such a brave thing. I was scared of my shadow; scared of branches crashing down on me; scared of the magpies that seemed to glower from their tree: 'This is our place.' I thought they hated me.

Now, after these seven sweet years of transplant success, I thrill at the sight of magpies fighting off eagles, their courage and skill, whole families soaring and swooping in defence of their territory. I kiss this teeming, lively earth with a deepening gratitude every day. But no matter the names on the mortgage papers, no matter the lengths of fencing wire, this place is not really mine. It's not my *home*.

Home for me is a house to live in, write in, sleep in, a temporary stopping point on the way from wherever I've been to wherever it is I'm going. Like a dandelion seed, I've let the weather take me, a white wisp drifting to all soils. A random, timeless fairy clock, and a weed, no matter how pretty my flowers might appear. A field of Paterson's curse is breathtakingly gorgeous—a violet carpet rolling across picture-book hills—and it's toxic. Between me and the tree, colonies of butter-yellow cape daisies compete with clover and the spindly stalks of ungrazed phalaris pasture. Periwinkle chicory blossoms dance on warm squalls above native everlastings, robbing them of light. Where did all these weeds come from? Everywhere—every continent on earth.

I am a creature of diaspora, of rivers of people streaming around the globe. Economic migrants escaping the poverty of 1890s Tralee, scrambling over the dead to grab their tickets for the next ferry, and others waving too-ra-loo to the Yiddish-speaking streets of London's East End on their way through from Baltic Germany and Europe's ever more violent anti-Semitism. People wanting something somewhere better. None of them were saints or remotely noble. My Irish great uncles, with no education or prospects to harness clever minds, ran illegal gambling dens in Surry Hills and Lewisham, while my Jewish family tree is stacked with drunks and bankrupts, frauds and thieves. I treasure the Hebrew script of my great-great-great-grandmother's marriage certificate; I treasure the scandalous, far-fetched legend that she ran off to goldrush Melbourne with her husband's best mate even more. No wonder I'm a novelist.

The tree of my life bursts with colour, with incredible tales of daring and luck. A series of chances taken by desperate gamblers, dodging famines and pogroms, getting away before the Troubles and the Holocaust could lop the branches that made me.

The stories that brought me to this place.

Peace whispers through gum leaves with the simplest truth: 'You don't belong here.'

I don't. None of my stories are of *here*, this place, no matter how many stories I write about its people, landscapes, heartscapes. Trees.

In *Bila Yarrudhanggalangdhuray,* Anita's Heiss's sumptuous Wiradjuri saga—in English, *River of Dreams*—the heroine, Wagadhaany, explains to her two little sons that their beloved aunty hugs a redgum because she is giving her love and gratitude to the tree for the bark it supplies. I gave no such stories of Country-nourished grace to my sons when they were small.

I can read 'The Dictionary of Albert Goondiwindi' from Tara June Winch's soul-mapping masterpiece, *The Yield,* and find the Wiradjuri words for 'kidneys' and 'red gum tree' but I can't say them, or write them here. They don't belong to me.

My name is not of this place. My birth name, my family name, Swivel, is a fiction itself, anglicised from Schwebel during World War

One—to avoid anti-German hatred or the stain of my great grandfather's bad debts, take your pick, but either way I'm saddled with a vaguely amusing, vaguely embarrassing name from nowhere. I write under the penname Kelly, my mother's family name, to avoid the long and unresolvable story. To disappear and reappear as something somehow familiar. More easily marketable.

I was raised to think of myself as nothing from nowhere, too. My Irish grandmother called my brother and me 'bitzers'—bits of this and bits of that—and my parents were backyard-barbeque internationalists who didn't believe in Australia long before it was fashionable to do so. No 'God Save the Queen' in our house, no flags or allegiances beyond rugby league teams; and when I was asked to identify myself at school—'what are you, Aussie or Wog?'—I replied, 'Nothing,' and didn't consider that to be a negative.

Growing up at La Perouse, on the axe-edge northern stretch of Botany Bay, my first friends were of the First Nations, of Bidjigal, Gadigal and Yuin. My oldest childhood comrade in story-love and laughter, a Saltwater woman from the sapphire coast, has always shown me how wonderful it is that our histories have been able to meet and mesh in truth and light. But these beyond-the-mountains Wiradjuri leaves continue to whisper and whisper anyway:

'You don't belong here.'

I know. *I know*. But where else can I go?

Fear is a feather trembling within the core of my heart. Beneath the colour and quips of family history and mystery, there are grey, fraying threads of depression, of failure to thrive, and suicides, two of them, interweave the Kellys and the Schwebels together, ghosts at my parents' wedding. Their fathers each lost a brother: one hung himself; the other jumped off the Gap. Why? Was it this unbelonging? A curse of trespass?

This land is scarred by me, by my house and my ripening plums and tomatoes; this land is forever changed by my invasion. Can't gather back the seeds.

And yet, from its kitchen-window frame, the tree outside looks down at me with lofty indifference, shrinking my shallow-rooted vanity.

The sun rises, the kettle boils. I have work to do, debts to make good, in the only currency of worth I have: my words.

◆

A kidney looks just as much like a giant seed as it does a tree. A seed that's perpetually sprouting. A magic bean promising poor Jack a stalk that'll take him up through the clouds to steal back the riches he's owed. But no one is owed a kidney. Transplantation of this magic bean is a small but epic journey of luck in itself.

The latest stats from the Australian Institute of Health and Welfare say there are around 15,000 kidney patients on renal dialysis, a system by which the blood is artificially filtered, most commonly through an intravenous machine. Dialysis does a more or less adequate job of helping people stay alive, but it's not a permanent solution; it's tough on the body, never getting the balance of minerals and fluids quite right, so that patients are often increasingly bone-weary from slow poisoning, not to mention the constantly disruptive rigmarole of the process, which usually involves several hours hooked up in hospital every second day. There's no cure for end-stage renal failure, only dialysis, and, if fortune is on your side, transplant. In 2021, only 857 transplants were performed—some 14,000 less than needed. Even taking into account the interruptions to all surgical lists caused by the Covid-19 pandemic, that's quite a gap between supply and demand. Of these transplants, only 24% were sourced from living donors—like me. Which means, obviously, that most kidneys came from people who had died. A precious gift of life for one; and the ultimate sacrifice for another.

Potential deceased-donor kidney recipients are added to a waiting list, all hanging on the call that will tell them when it's time to dash to the hospital for their transplant. A call that can take as long as seven years to come. It's not a simple matter of next cab off the rank: blood and tissue types need to be matched for compatibility; you need to have remained well enough to survive the surgery, too—and for the kidney to survive within you. No one gets to choose race or creed, no kosher, halal or vegan options exist, but genes do play a part—as does access to treatment.

Westmead's Centre for Kidney Research figures show that First Nations Australians in particular are ten percent less likely to be added to the transplant list, because of a combination of delays in diagnosis and dialysis, general governmental negligence of Aboriginal health, and the mechanics of structural racism. Many First Nations patients die waiting a long way from their Country, and some return to Country preferring to die more gently there.

I've seen for myself the lack of understanding Aboriginal dialysis patients routinely receive, medical staff talking about them and their 'non-compliance' with treatment schedules as if they're not in the room. I tried to tell one young guy with my eyes that I was ashamed at the way he'd been insulted by a nurse after missing a few days for a family funeral, but he wouldn't look at me, and who could blame him? My shame might have been more useful if I'd told that nurse she should show some respect. And common sense: Wiradjuri Country is vast, a nation bigger than Ireland and Wales combined, and both dialysis wards he might have attended were likely miles from where he had needed to be. Why wouldn't you want to spend some precious days with your grieving family? We're all a long time dead.

Why didn't I say something?

Fear: that it wasn't my place to speak. Irrational fear: that if I made a fuss, put someone offside, Deano and I might miss our transplant date. Miss *our* chance. This is the insidiousness of structural racism—a medical system always under pressure, patients grasping for whatever they can get, making silent excuses for why some are placed last in the race to live—and the proof of it is written on my soul.

Privilege wrote a happy ending for me. After jumping through a series of death-defying test-tube hoops, jumping at all my shadows through ultrasounds and cardio charts, I could hardly believe it when I wasn't diagnosed with a terminal illness myself, and it turned out that my A+ blood was a near enough match for Deano's O. His blood would have to be whirled through another machine to strip it of antibodies to mine, but apart from that we were ready to go.

'What an adventure!' I shouted fairy tales at my two grown sons, lying like all our lives depended on it.

As I prepared for our big day, I read and wrote as though my own life depended on fiction alone, a fortress made of pages. I finished writing one novel, pressing send to the publisher; then, within a breath, began another. And in the night, under laptop light, I burrowed into Goethe's tiny, two-hundred-year-old poem, *Gefunden*:

Once through the forest
Alone I went;
To seek for nothing
My thoughts were bent,

I saw i' the shadow
A flower stand there;
As stars it glisten'd,
As eyes 'twas fair,

I sought to pluck it,—
It gently said:
'Shall I be gather'd
Only to fade?'

With all its roots
I dug it with care,
And took it home
To my garden fair,

In silent corner
Soon it was set;
There grows it ever,
There blooms it yet.

Nurturing my one Christmas wish: please, let my little bunch of roses bloom in the garden of my love.

Now, *Gefunden* reads more as an inadvertent allegory for white supremacist entitlement. See here, little flower, let me gather you up, remove you from where you were perfectly content and put you in a place of my choosing. For my pleasure and convenience.

To keep the wolves of grief at bay.

To feel powerful, triumphant, even within our tenderest vulnerabilities.

Kidney donation certainly does deliver some interesting contradictions and ethical ambiguities. Five months after the transplant, when my fourth novel was published, and I was still silly as loose balloon, as part of the publicity run I was asked to chat about how a girl might combine writing books and gifting organs, like so many childcare tips and easy, budget-friendly recipes. One journalist asked if I had any 'hospital selfies' I could send to them: 'You know, like before and after shots?' No, sorry, I could only reply, we weren't in the mood for that sort of thing at the time—for freak's sake. Further afield and more recently, US author and living donor Dawn Dorland had her real-life kidney story plundered by another writer and twisted into a tale of actual white supremacist entitlement: in short, weird white lady gives organ to grumpy not-white lady and, in a needy, white-saviour y way, asks for praise—as you do. It was all laid bare in the *New York Times* 2021 article 'Who is the Bad Art Friend?', and erupted into a literary Twitter storm so vile it was hard to believe that at its centre was the gift of a little pink kidlet.

Maybe there's something icky about the offal aspect to it all, and about transplant generally, something Frankensteinish that we don't like to talk about in loving terms. The harvesting and grafting of body parts—well, ew. Hospital gowns spattered with the rose-red blood of new life don't quite make us feel warm and fuzzy inside. But then, what do I know about romance? The heroine of that fourth novel was compelled to gruesomely murder her tormentor in the ghost-strewn Bathurst hills before the path of her true love could hope to run smooth. Maybe I'd been dealing with some psychological issues—just a few—tapping out terror in code, white-knuckled, grasping for courage. Desperate.

In the sleepless dark, I still wonder and wonder, is transplantation unnatural God-playing, or is it a sublime, medically enhanced sacrament of giving and receiving?

It is loss and gain by a few deft scratches of a blade. It is brutal: a caesarean slash across the base of my belly, a numbness there still; the keyhole chinks above still visible under my ribs.

Nietzsche, that old bundle of neurotic paradoxes, said of his own baffling illness that it gave him 'a higher kind of health, a sort of health which grows stronger under everything that does not actually kill it'. Illness is a teacher, a scope through which we can examine our lives, and become wiser, maybe more empathetic—when we're not having a crap day. But it's also a place we long to escape once we're stuck there. We all want to be well, whatever wellness means to each of us. And when someone we love is dying, it's no leap of logic that some of us, given the chance and the choice, will do whatever it takes.

Maybe one day transplant surgeries will seem as crude and wrong as colonialism itself. But for now, for me, it's a daily waking to bright blue eyes; it's hearing Deano's ute coming down our potholed track at dusk, his key in the door; his kiss. It is magic. Miraculous. Human and beautiful. Perhaps a healing seed of story. Not gift or receipt, but something to share.

Kim Kelly is author of thirteen long-form fictions. Her work has been short, and longlisted for various awards, and her latest novella, *Ladies' Rest and Writing Room*, won the 2023 Finlay Lloyd 20/40 Prize. She holds a Master of Creative Writing from Macquarie University, for which she earned the Faculty of Arts Fred Rush Convocation Prize, and she's currently undertaking a Creative Writing PhD there. Because too much narrative action is never enough, she also works as a book editor.

Blood, Phlegm, Yellow Bile, Black Bile

OR

The Story of How My Sibling and I Time-Travelled to Kill God

Yazmin Bradley

I pray you, be content, 'tis but his humour.
Shakespeare, *Othello* Act 4, Scene 2

◆

The Physician will ask that the two bodies be placed upon twin tables. The bodies are accompanied by two villagers who claim to be their parents; the latter are sickly, poor, scabbed mouths hidden by woollen shrouds. They have come far to find this Physician. He is the best of his kind. The parents have asked for a miracle, the bodies are not dead, but they soon will be and they're not picky. A measly coin is pressed into his hand: there is the rancid hope of beatification, ghastly Sainthood if these bones and flesh can perform wonders so let's give it a good go while they breathe their last. It's good for business. The Physician orders the bodies be stripped—he does not bother washing them, and what for? It is the Humours that are the problem. Let the flesh putrefy, he thinks. A little rot never hurt the female body.

He checks their tongues first, then peels back their lids, peers into brown and blue glass. He could spit on their eyes and see his teeth in the reflection, but that would be blasphemous and there is measly coin to collect for the farce of respect. And so, the charade continues. Blood, phlegm, yellow bile, black bile. These two are out of balance in biblical proportions. One has too much phlegm, the other not enough. Black bile bleeding into yellow. Infected blood, scum on top of a broth pot.

'I'll have to bleed them,' he wheezes and leers at the bodies with yellow teeth. He fingers each rusted instrument with deep reverence. Out of his medical kit he pulls a cracked dish, crooks it under the arm of the first body. Cadaver the Elder. He makes it look like practical consideration but it's more a case of tossing a measly coin. He doesn't know their names. They arrived to him like this—listless, lifeless, which is understandable since they are already dead. There will be no beatification, no Sainthood, he knew this from the start. But robbing these folk is good for business. And so, the charade continues.

'Be not afraid, madam,' he says to the shorter one in the shroud. She is moustachioed like her husband. 'This will ease their suffering.'

And he skewers the child like a pig, although this is a mistake because the study of Pallor mortis hasn't been invented yet and there is little explanation for what happens—or doesn't—other than the Devil. The Mother murmurs, moves forward in a stupor, tries to snatch the empty dish. Where is the blood? Where is the promised miracle? The charade is somewhat thwarted.

'Too much yellow bile!' he cries, waving her away. 'It clots the blood but only in the left side of the body. The feminine side. I must attempt the other vein.'

He carries on like this for a while, puncturing the bodies with vigour. The blood has congealed, the children are waxen and cold, the stiffness has set in. The latent miracle has calcified. It is a rotten dead thing. The measly coin spent, spoiled business. The Mother has fainted, the Father has stumbled away although he returns with a Priest, a harried young man who smells of sour milk.

'I did what I could.'

Clack, clack, clack, go his yellow teeth—he pockets the coin—and the sour Priest wrings his hands. It is a full moon tonight and he's on burning duty.

'But it appears our Good Lord had other plans for them,' he adds.

'Indeed,' says the Priest impatiently and he raises his hand with an economic jerk, blessing undesirables is beneath him, but he spots something. A mark on the elder's body, just below the womb. The miracle manifest? Stigmata? The Priest snaps his finger at the Physician.

'Bring me that candle. Quickly, now.'

The candle is brought close to the body, close to the cool, pallid skin.

'Physician, do you see that?'

'Aye, Father.'

A rational hypothesis is the Witch's mark. No need to corroborate the other body—although for the reader's convenience both legs are marked. The Priest straightens and calls for wood and oil which takes longer than it should since grieving parents are rather useless. The full moon is pregnant and the bodies thrown heavily onto the pyre.

It's a quick affair and only a scattered crowd but that can be improved with a little time and effort, the sour Priest thinks. His career is still young, after all. Blood, phlegm, yellow bile, black bile. The Father drinks himself to sleep and the Mother throws herself off a cliff—business is bad, remember? The Physician fingers his measly coin, and the Priest fills his quota, and the two bodies burn, happily.

And so, the charade continues.

◆

It is an effort to drag myself from the wreckage but since I am the eldest, I need to show You the way. Soot-stained, ashen mouth. I look better than You since your blue eyeball has dribbled down your face. Shame. On a scale of violence, we'll grant the sour Priest a four—the scale goes to nine hundred and thirty-six, for reference. I will retrieve This Century's Mother from the bottom of the cliff. You will fetch Imitation Father from the pub. We'll put them to bed and tuck them in and then we'll murder the Priest and Physician. A double homicide. We'll skewer and roast them, suck the rot from their bones, knit ourselves back together, slowly.

Flesh is good, marrow is better, although a bit of measly coin gets stuck in my new teeth. The marks don't go away, we haven't figured that bit out yet, although my marks are much smaller than yours.

There's an incision in my belly button where I was impaled, another three which cradle my lower belly. I was cleaved only once when I came of age but I have begged them since to do it again. What pig asks to be barbecued twice? You have been cleaved three times now—*thrice the brinded cat hath mew'd*—long pink ridges down the back of your calves like stocking seams—*thrice and once the hedge-pig whined*—another parallel to the knee, and still there is a fourth to come—*Harpier cries 'Tis time, 'tis time.*

And it is time, I suppose, although that is entirely dependent on how much money one has to throw at the problem, and we have never had enough of that which is why we are here in the filth of the sixteenth century. Nasty place. We have been burned four times now which is getting rather dull but it's a means to an end and the end is in sight—we are on our way to kill God. And since we are going backwards—or forwards, depending on your concept of Time—things start to get strange. Time overlaps. And Time is not so much of a continuum than it is a palimpsest of scar tissue, a book that fattens with infection, grows pregnant with blood. It smells of bone—it smells like You. It smells of iron—it smells like Me.

Me is made up back to front. A user manual gone rogue. For readers who like a bit of light science—Physician, look away—I am a composite of targets called autosomes. Twenty-two of them. The twenty third is the sex chromosome and it is three times larger than the male counterpart. A target so much the bigger. My internal sex organs form from the gelatinous ridges of tissue that spurt from my infantile abdomen—and then comes all the Naughty bits. Clitoral hood/uterus/womb/labia minora/urethral opening/Fallopian tubes/breasts/nipples/vagina—note for sixteenth century readers, all facets of the female reproductive system are conveniently translated to Cunt. But there's something about my uterus, a rogue stitch, a knot gone wrong, webs of dark red tissue dangling from the needles, because the tissue that should be lining my uterus is naughty. It's not in its right place.

It first started with the bleeding; the lining of the uterus builds like a dam ready to catch a fertilised egg, cradle it, warm it—except when there is no fertilised egg the lining breaks down and bleeds. Stock standard, case closed. Except there's the naughty lining again, endometrial tissue, out of bed at this hour! It grows like a tumour; it grows like mould. Endometriosis cakes my bowels, pollinates my kidneys, suffocates my organs. At least, in theory. Physicians checked everywhere except the places where endometriosis grows which means they checked nowhere. According to them I should be fine at the bleeding. Pain since time immemorial, pain since normal, pain since Eve—this is why we are killing God.

But pain at the bleeding turns my hair white. Pain at the bleeding makes trophies of my ivory knuckles. Pain at the bleeding blanches my bones.

We have wasted too much time here, You say. Time to move on to the thirteenth century, the budding flower of all disease—which came first, God or Rot? We swim through the ichor, it slicks us like oil until we pierce the watery membrane of Time and gasp, breathe in the stench of fear and confusion. The air is wet with the sickly sweetness of pus, the bloody tang of iron. Engorged nodules cling lovingly to armpits, lymph nodes swell like the tide, rashes cling to scabbed necks—these people are devotees to suffering like long-term lovers, they are architects of reason—lucky them. They know why they are suffering. It is more cellular than the humours in the thirteenth century. Sin goes straight to the bone.

It starts with the atom: an infected flea, plague bacillus enters the bite and traverses the lymphatic system like a European skier before it breaks its fast at the lymph node, splits and divides itself. The lymph node becomes a bubo, it becomes tense, a little peeved. It gets so angry it mutates into an open sore, fills itself with pus. But it is smart, it comes with a sibling—And God saw the light, that it was good: and God divided the light from the darkness: yersinia pestis infiltrates the lungs and severs the cell's comms. It strands the cell, a lone lamb bleating for help. It can take up to seven days for death—And on the seventh day God ended His work which He had made.

I covet the explanation, the fleas, the germs, the sin, the quick suffering. You covet relief, mobility, ease, which is why we are here.

There is an Alchemist by the river—the river is filled with shit—who treats the sick and the dying.

She lives in a hut. Pretty shit place for the King's alchemist but then You suppose the feudal system does put a dampener on the whole thing. She greets us outside which is a nice change. Witch burning kicks off in about three months, so we still have time. She isn't as worried as she should be. Inside the house on the packed earthen floor, she lays You on a cot stuffed with straw. I can see in your eyes You want to complain but she pulls up your trouser cuffs, inspects your scars and clicks her tongue.

'These scars art deep,' she says. 'What w're thy physicians looking f'r?'

I can see You thinking and You give me a look, I shrug. We're not here for the diagnosis, only the treatment. But it doesn't hurt to give the woman context.

Mine legs cannot breathe, You reply. Mine legs art strangl'd things.

It's always an exercise in creativity translating incurable conditions. I say condition because You are in somewhat of a liminal state, the place between breaths. You say 'strangl'd' because it is the closest Early Modern English word to Asphyxiate: i.e. to be unable to breathe; to suffocate. Your calf muscle is in the wrong place which means it presses on the artery, makes it difficult for blood to flow to your legs. When you walk your feet glow like steel fresh from the crucible. They are calcified, dead things. In Modern English it has been termed Popliteal artery entrapment syndrome but that's a mouthful. Father just called it lazy.

The Alchemist tuts again, turns your ankles. Pinches your calves and You blanche.

'The binding of thy ankles helps naught,' she says, but we knew that already.

Scar tissue underneath the skin. Disappointment is branded between the sinew of your muscles and the best doctors in the country cannot heal that charred flesh.

Walking bringeth ye pain and yet ye p'rsist?

I take this opportunity to give You a look that needs no translation: I told You so. But I know why You do it, even if it brings me pain to see. Your legs are a farmyard complication and Father shoots lame horses. Compromise, Mother said. Instead, he strapped your ankles, bit and tackle, handed you the whip. Father is long dead, but You haven't taken them off.

Your face is answer enough. The Alchemist nods, thinks for a moment, then:

'There is nay cure.'

Her response isn't a surprise, we have been here before but in a different time and those doctors didn't live in huts and practise the Royal Art. They drove BMWs. They wore nice watches and lived on the North Shore. They were on two hundred-thousand-dollar salaries.

You stand, wince with pain. You haven't rested enough; I'll have to make sure we don't wade through Time for too long. I make a note to carry You through the hard parts. We move to leave but she looks at me shrewdly.

A pestilence is in thy womb.

We thank the Alchemist for her time and leave her hut by the stinking river in the heat of the summer that will kill a third of the world. Twelfth century? I offer. You suggest the sixth.

It hasn't always been like this, us crawling through history. There's been periods of loneliness, of silence. We fought after I murdered Freud, your birthday present to me. I tried to give You yours while my hands were still sticky. Instead, I didn't hear from You for years, not till Napoleon strode across Russia to the hollow belly of Moscow. I found You there, astride a horse dressed in the uniform of a Polish Winged Hussar. I told You to stop being silly, to get off the horse. You're play-acting, I said. It's childish, the uniform didn't even fit properly. I thought You would listen, heed me. Instead, You told me to go fuck myself.

'Was it Freud?' I asked. Of course, it wasn't Freud.

I admit I probably shouldn't have gifted You the cane. It was meant to be a birthday present, there in Freud's office. Managed to squirrel it out of WWII. Stole it off an Englishman with medals on his lapel and a full head of hair. The cane was hawthorn, lacquered, its head a dragon's maw snarling. I watched him hobble around that old Georgian monstrosity with it. Watched him beat his servants with it. So I stole it.

I thought You would be grateful. Instead, You threw it at me and shouted, stormed away. I followed. You aren't beneath using a cane, I said. You aren't beneath being a cripple. Was I talking to You or to me? Perhaps I went too far because that was the last time we spoke for one hundred and twenty-seven years. And when I finally found You in the bowels of the cavalry dressed in that ridiculous, magnificent costume, I wanted to tear You down from the horse, lame it. I wanted to force the cane that I had lugged with me for a century into your hand. I wanted to say that your pride makes me want to start a war. Your pain makes me want to steal from cripples.

If humiliation is the price of relief let me pay it for You. I can bear your hatred.

Instead I said nothing at all, threw the cane into the snow. I offered You my hand and helped You climb down the horse's flank, removed the bit and tackle. Returned the whip. We walked away, slowly. I let You lean on my arm. We took little breaks.

We sold the uniform nearby, used the cash to take a sled and a pack of dogs into Siberia but You kept the wings. I couldn't deprive You of that and when we stopped for camp, I gave You a larger portion of the dried meat even though my belly ached. I took first watch, and as you rolled over, I wondered if You were flying in your sleep.

We cycle through Time quickly now, speed-reading I call it. We decide to skip Jesus—we're so close to the Source now—the self-sanctimonious martyr. I can't tell which disgusts me more; the fact that he would dilute his love amongst so many undeserving, or that pain is the only way to elevate love. I would not die for a thousand people, and I would never voluntarily choose pain. We steal a glance at Golgotha on our way to the top, watch throngs of people gather around the man who is the son of God—You are sceptical. We see his hands caked in blood, watch the Romans look on smugly. A mother is weeping, probably

Mary, and for a moment I am disappointed. What are three days of pain compared to a lifetime? If it were You on the cross, I would rip You down and nail my hands to the wood myself. If it were You on the cross, I would choose pain eternal.

Perhaps my first assessment of Jesus was unfair.

As a special request, we make a stop with the Ancient Greeks. You make a good case for philosophy, argue that perhaps we don't need to kill God at all—the Greeks can think their way through pain. It's bullshit, we both know, but I humour You regardless. I am hesitant, what will I do here but languish? They have no need for me in their symposiums. But You are like the colour that oil makes on water: iridescence, an ever-present process of alchemy. For You, space and time are less binaries than spectrums. You tell me not to be afraid and You carry me into the city on your back.

Aristotle is an excellent host although his idea to act as tour guide is somewhat less appreciated especially since it mostly involves eating and drinking and discoursing and these are all things that act as kindling for the endometrial tissue that lines my insides like dynamite. Travel, even time-travel, is a stressor on the body. You, however, are as happy as a pig in shit; the pressure is off your legs, there are attendants here to take care of all aches and pains—unpaid, obviously—although it does seem cruel that you can only watch the satyrs dancing for Dionysus. It would be nice to join rapture and oblivion. And since Stagira is beautiful this time of year and the grapes are fat and the oil is like silk and the meat runs thick with juices and the night bleeds ink over the sky, we stay.

Halfway through the feast it starts, a bubble bubble. A quickening in my belly, the fermentation of something sour although it's been brewing for a while, toil and trouble. Suddenly the oil shimmering on bare skin smells rancid and fair is foul and foul is fair. My own body feels slick and engorged like a fat snake. My cheeks are too hot and it's not because an orgy has started in the next room. I hover through the smoke and filthy air.

'Are you well?' a woman asks, but I wave her away.

A seed has germinated in my brain, a white-hot seed, it makes a high-pitched keening sound and I gasp.

Let me help you, the woman says, putting her hands under my armpits to drag me somewhere but I smack her hands, speak your name, ask for drugs.

She looks blankly at me, at my bloodied dress. I can't translate drugs to medicine because what I've asked for is not medicine. It's oblivion. You are the gatekeeper of obliteration, so I try to translate You. It takes a couple of goes but she gets it in the end. She leaves me alone in the feast room, panting like a dog. When You finally arrive with the drugs followed by Aristotle—*something wicked this way comes*—my knuckles are in my mouth, and they're covered in blood.

'Water,' You snap at someone.

From white packaging You produce a white pill, force it down my throat and water board me with the pitcher—*What's done cannot be undone.*

'Why didn't you take this earlier?'

Pant pant gasp. I don't know. I can tell You're angry with me.

'Why didn't you have the pills on you?'

'Thought it wouldn't happen. Didn't need it.'

'That's stupid.'

If I weren't lying prostrate on the floor begging Apollo to gut me, I would have screamed. You're always acting older than You are, it's insufferable. Why won't You accept that you're a child? The ink-bleed sky is clouded with fat and scum. The little pill has done its work.

The sound of safety foil being punctured makes You look up but it's too late. Aristotle has pushed one into his mouth. You're so furious You forget to speak Ancient Greek. The translation: My tongue will tell the anger of my heart, or else my heart concealing it will break. There were only two tablets left and now one is wasted. One tablet between two children, one tablet until the end of Time. And how can we choose between us? Whatever You say doesn't matter, the pills work quicker this close to the Source and Aristotle sits heavily, legs splayed like a child. His eyes are glassy.

Surrender to sleep, he says. What a misery, keeping watch through the night, wide awake. His words are slurred, and we ignore him. There's not enough pity to spare. You hoist me off the floor. I'm limp like a rag doll, and You cradle my head in your lap. I have soiled myself, but You don't say anything.

Let us both pretend I am not ashamed. Let us both pretend I don't want You to grow up. Let us both pretend I am still the elder sibling.

And so, the charade continues.

Killing God ends up being a small affair. I won't waste time explaining how we got Here since there wasn't much Here to begin with. We rip Him apart quickly and efficiently, scatter him like ashes to sea. Clack clack clack go his yellow teeth into some pocket of a star. Over his eyes we place measly coins. From his brain we harvest the atom, the seed, genesis. Give it a shake, a hard reset. When that doesn't fix it, we split it asunder, cleave it, skewer it, drill down into the nexus of pain.

At the bottom of the well is a question mark—Who do you say I am? We are disappointed—What must I do to be saved? In hindsight we should have killed Apollo, he would have at least dignified us with an answer. You call God a cop out; even He isn't sure of the point of all this. So then what is the use of the scriptures? It's an anomaly in the code of the universe, like your legs, like my womb. A giant question mark, no cure, no reason. God desperate for an answer.

There's a power struggle over who gets to snap the ambivalence in half. Over who has more claim. 'Me,' I say: I am the eldest. You explode with righteous anger, You have every right, but You misunderstand me. I don't want the sin because I think You cannot bear it. I am the one who cannot bear it. I should make Jesus look weak, I should carry all the sins of the world upon my back for You, but I can't. My exhaustion is too great. The last little pill has done its work again. Your hand closes around mine.

I can do nothing but let You take it; watch You annihilate the world into a million pieces for after all it is only just for God to repay with affliction those who afflict you, and to give relief to You who are afflicted. Standing hurts your legs, your bare feet are bone white, but I can't do anything to help You. What's the point of God's waiting room if there isn't even a chair? I prostrate on the floor again, asking oblivion to gut me as the naphtha flash of creation reversing blinds me, and there is no longer any sea, and I sleep.

In the beginning You create the heavens and the earth.

There is no wreckage to drag ourselves from, there is only Nothing. The earth is a formless void and darkness covers the face of the deep. It was the only way we could get rid of pain, to snuff life itself, rewire the code, start again. The scars are still there, but You show me how You moulded your calf muscle like bloodied clay, free the asphyxiated arteries with an audible hiss. You have done so much while I was sleeping. You have aged too, or perhaps You were always this old because You wash my feet, turn water into wine. And then You show me how to cauterise my endometrial tissue, cool the inflammation of my insides like dousing a bush fire. For You, it's easy stuff. Playthings. A child playing dress up with creation. You're wearing the wings. My little sibling working miracles.

Perhaps neither of us is the eldest or the youngest. Perhaps we simply take turns like the sun and the moon. Like dawn and dusk. Like blood, phlegm, yellow bile, black bile.

In the beginning, there is only us.

Yazmin Bradley is a writer of the weird and the strange. From Western Sydney on unceded Dharug Land, Yazmin holds a double degree in International Relations and Media (Screen & Sound Production) from UNSW. She is currently pursuing her Master of Creative Writing with Macquarie University. Her writing has been published in *The Suburban Review*.

JUVENILE

Tedi Symons

It's 2007, and in a quiet suburb of southern Sydney a pair of peppermint gums loom over a family home seated in the middle of a long street, ironically called Shorter Avenue. Under the shade of those tall gums, a trio of kids run around with wild abandon until one falls, unbalanced by their knobbly knees knocking together. They are sent sprawling across the grass unnoticed by the others. It seems to hurt more than a simple stumble should. After unsteadily scrambling to their feet, the curly headed child begins to shuffle into the house, lip quivering and eyes quickly welling up with tears.

Inside, the solid thump of a closing door interrupts the diligent cleaning of a young mother. She hears the uneven steps of an unusual gait as it echoes down the hallway. Her concern sends her out of her room to meet them. Down the length of the hall she can see her usually excitable child is in tears; immediately worried, she scans them for any signs of injury. At seven years old, her youngest is somewhat oddly shaped. While not overtly obvious, it's clear as day to her trained eye—over the past year since the diagnosis, it's become easier and easier for her to spot the abnormalities.

She wished that they had never appeared.

Under the riot of curly dark hair they're skinny—their legs, alongside small feet, smaller hands, and a slightly undersized chin—have earnt them the nickname, 'Pippi Longstocking'. She despairs how their features add up to a body on which it is *literally* child's play to see the obnoxious swellings that plague their still-growing joints. They stiffly totter towards her with straight legs—their inflamed knees unable to bend. When the pair meet in the middle, those stick-thin limbs—akin to the knotted twigs that the gums overhead often drop in the yard—are brandished, thrust towards her as evidence of the tumble they'd taken; even as she realises the light grazes are hardly the source of their plaintive whine, 'Mummy, my knees hurt.'

She's honestly a little surprised—despite the pain she knows is always there, her youngest isn't one to complain. There's a part of her that wonders if they've even realised that everyone else doesn't have to deal with the same chronic aches.

She crouches, gathering them up in a tight embrace and gently brushing their curls aside to get a good look at them. The young mother gathers herself, knowing there's nothing she can really do right now to fix the internal hurt. She instead smacks an overly dramatic kiss to their small, sweaty forehead before leaning back to inspect the offending joints.

On bad days like these, each of their knees is so inflamed her fingertips have no chance of meeting each other when she wraps her hands around the swollen bulk. Nevertheless, she rubs each carefully between her palms and raises their legs to bestow both knees with their own individual kisses. Putting on a big smile, she declares the pain vanquished—after all, she's 'kissed it all better' now. Before her eyes, the tears dry up and a blinding smile splits the young face, dimples pinching deep into the only fat that lingers in those childishly chubby cheeks. She keeps all the tumultuous emotions that writhe in her chest locked up tight until her child turns away, employing that strange straight-legged gait once more to hobble off down the hall. Momentarily placated from the ache, they're clearly eager to get out and play again.

When they're out of sight she stands and walks back into her bedroom, softly closing the door behind her and slumping onto the bed. Burying her face in her hands, she cries.

◆

Weatherbone

Cast the weather from my bones.
Ribs, rattled by the wind.
Skull, split by shards of sun.
Knees, injected with clouds.
Joints, bogged down but unsound;
Filled with weightless fluid—
Too heavy to move,
Too gaseous to hold strong.

Creeping cold is a thief, stealing my energy—
I am being siphoned through my marrow.
Prop me up amongst the other taxidermies;
Existing long past their time,
Hollow boned and
Stuffed with the atmosphere.

◆

In 2006, I was little more than just another rambunctious six-year-old who happened to be a bit prone to illness. During one such bout of sickness, my mum happened to ask our family GP about something abnormal she had begun to notice, almost as an afterthought. Every now and then my joints would suddenly inflate, aching and swelling with seemingly no rhyme or reason. Initially, she had just assumed the problem came from how often it was for me to trip and skin my knees, but the inflammation persisted long after any scrapes had healed. Unknown to my mum at the time, this simple question would be the beginning of our complex understanding of Juvenile Idiopathic Arthritis—JIA for short.

At first, the very idea of this diagnosis was baffling; my parents didn't know arthritis was something a kid could even *get*, having always heard of it as something that comes after injury or with age. In the Westmead Children's Hospital we met Dr Singh, the rheumatologist who would become the voice of expertise on my condition for years. He gave my parents the first real opportunity to understand what was going on in my body. However, it wasn't quite the reassurance they had hoped for. While the 'juvenile' in JIA is pretty self-explanatory, indicating that the disease is diagnosed primarily in children and teenagers, 'idiopathic' means *unknown*. Essentially, researchers can't point to a specific reason *why* kids get JIA, especially because the disease presents through multiple types, alongside any case-by-case differences.

Dr Singh explained that the JIA types are autoimmune or autoinflammatory rather than the 'wear-and-tear' arthritis my parents and the general populace were more familiar with, although they do share some symptoms—chiefly the inflammation and deterioration of joints. So, it turned out that alongside the pain, inflammation, weakness and stiffness, my frequent sickness was just another side-effect. When experiencing 'flare-ups' my immune system waged civil wars within me, causing fevers while the heavy medication I was on dealt out its own issues. The JIA persisted until I went into remission at eleven and my family were hopeful that would be the end of it. Unfortunately, the disease returned when I was sixteen with a vengeance as it spread to more joints.

Looking past the pain, sickness, mobility issues, and chronic exhaustion, one of the most difficult—or perhaps more aptly, one of the more *annoying*—aspects of my disability is the riptide of helplessness that lurks beneath the surface at all times. While the feeling can be managed, just like my condition (not cured—*never* cured—but managed) it tends to crash over me in waves of intensity that differ day-to-day. It's the lack of control over important aspects of my life—like my body, thoughts, even my aspirations—that threatens to tug me beneath the surface, overwhelming me. There is a constant internal battle raging between the necessity of independence versus the childlike desire to be taken care of. While I am not helpless, I feel like some part of me never quite grew up; forever juvenile.

My health and illness has always been intertwined with my relationship with my mum—mentioning this piece to her had her immediately reminiscing and asking whether I would want to interview her to ask for her perspective at any point, which is how the opening point-of-view came to be. She was the primary contact for my health all through my childhood, and she was still involved in my early adulthood; she even came with me to the first appointments with my new rheumatologist. I actually was treated by Dr Singh for longer than I technically should have because of the return of my arthritis in my late teens, which might have contributed to some lack of knowledge, formed by the security of being looked after and shielded from the idea that I was different from most people. Now, of course, this is not to put blame on anyone at all for the situation; it is certainly not the fault of my Mum or my doctors for not realising that I was woefully uninformed and did not myself think to ask for what I did not know.

◆

Doctored

Mouth closed, jaw locked, words trapped.
Am I unable to speak, or am I afraid to?
Is there more pain when I use it as an excuse,
Or am I just a hypochondriac?
Imagining symptoms, imagining solutions;
Maybe I should see a doctor every day—
All my symptoms will disperse into thin air.
I feel like it gets worse the more I stay quiet,
But it's too painful to speak.

◆

When I was eighteen and finally started going to appointments by myself as an 'adult', it was difficult to realise how little I knew about what was happening in my own body. It felt humiliating being faced with doctors asking questions I didn't have the answers to. Because, of course, they expected me to know everything; after all, it's been practically a lifelong condition. Having never learnt the true technicalities of my disease—especially after going into remission—I had no clue how to compare myself to 'regular' people, or even my past self. My ADHD doesn't exactly lead to great recall, so keeping track of my body has been fairly haphazard.

All I really knew was that the arthritis sucked when I was a kid, sucked when it came back in my teens, and it sucks now. Well ... that's if I can call it the same thing. You see, as JIA is something that presents during childhood, most of the information about it online is focused on guiding parents through the diagnosis stage and tends towards attempts at reassuring them that it's something that their kids could potentially grow out of. When you add that to the reality of having been one of those sick kids—wherein all of the information about your condition is mainly expressed from medical professionals directly to your parents, and any explanation given to you is watered down through metaphor—a lot of understanding seems to slip through the cracks.

Taking it upon myself to learn more was unfortunately disheartening. It was nigh impossible for me to find reliable information on how JIA presents in adults, with one the most helpful sites even stating that JIA is generally diagnosed as something else in adults, such as rheumatoid arthritis or spondylitis. My adult rheumatologist has listed me as having rheumatoid arthritis on the relevant forms instead of JIA in order to continue my medical support, even though I was never re-diagnosed and some of my existing symptoms don't exactly align. So, now I am an adult being impacted by *something*, having aged out of what my disease 'should' be, without having grown out of it. That's where the uncertainty begins to kick in and I am left feeling both old and young for different reasons.

I've often felt like a kid because of my inability to do certain things due to my ADHD-induced struggles with self-motivation coupled with the chronic exhaustion from my arthritis that only worsens on low mobility days. It's exhausting having people think you should just grow up and learn when they're tired of you not being able to do things that you physically and mentally cannot do, while at the same time dealing with other people infantilising you for those same reasons. And under all that, there's the remnants of the childhood wish to just be *normal*.

Sometimes the longing hits in unexpected ways; I shaved my hair recently and felt happier in myself for it, but I knew my mum was very against me doing so. However, she didn't tell me the reason why until after I'd done it—while I had been a sick kid, apparently I hadn't *looked* like a sick kid. She didn't have to say much more before I understood that she had believed through cutting my hair I would bring my illness into visibility in a way it hadn't ever really been, aside from the swelling and occasional braces and splints for my knees, wrists, and one stubborn pinky finger.

Perhaps, to her, I will always be that sick kid. When I am visibly or vocally unwell, I am not just her child, but a representation of the misplaced guilt and shame she's internalised all these years. It's a horrible curse—almost self-flagellating in nature—how my mum feels regret for something she had absolutely no control over, smothered by a strange grief for a life I could have lived. She speaks sometimes on how I was sick and swollen and in pain, but still smiling. Still pushing on. And I wonder if despite it all, that was the best version of me in her eyes. The one who pushed on, the one who believed themself better when gifted with a motherly kiss, the one who bounced back immediately. The one who didn't *look* sick.

I struggle to throw old batteries out these days; some sort of childish resistance to a self-made insecurity caused by how mum used to call me her 'double A battery'—because despite my arthritis and asthma I was a constant fount of ever-ready energy. Now that I'm older, we think the ADHD might've had a hand in that, but at the time she just thought it was how I expressed my boundless enthusiasm for life. The problem is, I think I've been pushing my battery far past capacity for a *long* time.

Honestly, I shame myself by insinuating that *she* could possibly feel ashamed because of me, of what I might be 'lacking'. Maybe it's the dregs of my own remorse and anxiety that lingers, an internalised ableism it has taken me nearly two decades to recognise and overcome. These misguided feelings spent a long time being fuelled by a fear I think resonates with every child who experiences that deep-rooted ache at the thought of being a disappointment. This phantom is more bone-deep than the inflamed battlefield of my joints, where it waits to burrow into the marrow and break open hollow bone at any perceived change in tone.

◆

Double A

Feeling like a battery run flat;
No more charge in my energy pack—
I've run out of juice,
And it's not something I can just produce.

I can't help but try,
Pushing myself more,
But it only leads me to fry—
It burns to my core.

I want to run and jump and sing,
I want to do each and every little thing.
But like the young prince's swan wing,
I feel only the sting of my nettle-wreathed limb.

While my ailment is less visible,
To me it feels equally as divisible—
What you can do I cannot,
Don't tell me you forgot.

◆

It is my somewhat philosophy-inspired belief that every person's experience of life is mediated through two key things: Language and Body. The way we define ourselves and the world around us depends on our reception of external and internal stimuli through our physical forms and through the words we use to understand what we receive.

And when you have a disconnect between the body's reception of stimuli and the language used to understand it—like one caused by a lack of knowledge—that definition of the self and the world which surrounds ... It becomes quite murky.

They used to teach me to think that *anything you can do, I can do too*. It's not bad to try and keep kids' hopes up, to be fair. But while I think they intended the message to be *anything you can do, I can do ... slightly differently,* or *with a little help,* I ended up internalising it as *anything you can do, I should be able to do, too*. Which, unfortunately, is not true. Even when I still consider myself to be lucky—*if I can walk and talk, I'm okay*—when I consider that I'm not as bad as I could be—*if I can walk for a little while and talk for a little while, I'm okay*—when I consider this as just the reality I have to live with—*I have to walk and talk through the pain, I have to be okay*—when I consider myself.

These days, I find it hard to consider my case when sometimes I'm not even sure *what* my case is. One of the hardest things, in my opinion, has been trying to outgrow the thought that *anything I can do, you can do better*. When you don't outgrow the disease, it can be a real challenge to try and outgrow the mindset.

◆

Fertiliser

Sometimes life piles shit onto you
And you just have to learn
To absorb the useful bits
And grow

In 2024, **Tedi Symons** graduated from Macquarie University's Master of Research with a thesis focusing on how fanfiction can be researched as a mode of contemporary digital literature. They have always had a passion for creative writing - usually focusing on fantasy, sci-fi, and romance. However, they also enjoy using their published poetry and non-fiction writing to share their perspective with others as a proud member of the LGBTQIA+ community who is neurodivergent, has a mixed heritage, and who has been diagnosed with multiple physical and mental conditions over the years.

His Eyes Are Red as Fire with Weeping

Kate Giles

My father was a mathematician, all straight lines and angles, closed cupboards and doors, always squaring things, a knife and fork, a book on a shelf. When he wasn't at university, he was in his garden, building walls and paths from stone collected from around the countryside. He was an Escher of sorts and the garden, his gallery. Down the back of the house, overlooking the reserve, he built a rounded brick mausoleum where his beloved goat is buried. The wall is shaped like the turret of a castle, curving in perfect symmetry.

One of the last pieces of rockwork dad built was a wall he promised Mum for her eightieth birthday. He was eighty-three years old, and his fine motor skills weren't what they had been, the mortar, not the clean finish of his earlier work, the rocks hazy and undefined. His determination though, was something to be admired. By then, Dad had been living with Parkinson's disease for over ten years and his sharp dexterity was whittling away.

◆

Mum used to say Dad had the hands of a surgeon. He was precise with everything he did from removing our childhood splinters to his immaculate handwriting that, although illegible to many, was a thing of beauty, a calligraphy full of even swirls and loops. He took on the role of hairdresser when we were kids and cut my older sister's hair, either in a perfect bowl or a severe angular helmet, exposing his love of geometry. He seemed to favour her straight hair over the kinks and curls of the rest of us—but perhaps it was simply that the shape of Dad's signature precision was only revealed in her hair and preserved forever in our old family photographs.

Mum would laugh at Dad's habit of matching pegs by colour to the items of washing as he hung them on the line, sheets and towels squared to keep their shape. He packed a suitcase like he was doing a jigsaw puzzle and the car for a holiday, like Tetris, no wasted space, all economy and still room for the four kids. Being a 'maths man' he loved telling us about the beauty of square numbers, perhaps, in hope we would inherit his packing skills, but more likely just to fuel our interest in his numerical passion. And though it failed to spark our enthusiasm at the time, something must have been kindled as two out of four of us went on to study mathematics at university.

Mostly a patient man, Dad loved nothing more than sitting at the dinner table surrounded by family; children, grandchildren and later great grandchildren, sharing one of mum's delicious meals. I remember as a kid sitting around the dinner table with the family, dad quiet and thoughtful, then suddenly he'd jump up, 'I've got it,' he'd exclaim as he rushed off to his study to scribble down the result of a maths problem he'd solved. He was an enigma to his children, who bumbled along, elbows on the table, concentrating only on the meal at hand.

There were only a few things Dad couldn't tolerate: the three s's; swearing, smoking and spilling. A few of us disappointed him with the first two—my sister and I caused chaos as teenagers, but anyone at all could accidentally spill a drink and lord help them if they did it at the dinner table, 'Everybody up!' Dad would yell furiously, seizing control and frantically clearing the table, mopping the spill and making a spectacular fuss about a wet tablecloth. His reaction was so out of proportion to the scale of the disaster, the rest of us would sit there eyeing each other trying not to laugh. I can only guess the spill unbalanced his equilibrium, his sense of order and distracted him from any chance of problem solving during that meal.

With major mishaps, though, Dad was calm. When one of his grandsons threw a ping pong bat through a window in a fit of anger and disappeared in fear of punishment, Dad eventually found him and sat him down calmly and said, 'We can replace a window, but we can't replace you, boyo,' and he hugged him tenderly.

◆

When our kids were little, we lived in an unconventional house in the bush. To get there you had to travel up a rocky three-kilometre track that took fifteen minutes to drive, or half an hour to walk. It was a forty-five-minute drive to the base of this track from town plus another four-hour drive for Mum and Dad from their house. Not an easy place to get to. I don't think Mum or Dad were particularly thrilled by our choice of habitat, but they would come and visit us, spend time with their grandchildren and help us around the place. We'd pick them up from the bottom of the hill or pick up their gear if they felt like a walk. They'd arrive with their air mattress and their sleeping bags for a few days and nights in the bush.

We grew vegetables, kept goats and chickens and were slowly building our house that we were living in as we built. There were few complete walls, our kitchen looked out to a vista of sweeping trees but there were no windows, just a sink, a bench and a wood fired stove, all roofed, but otherwise open to the elements. At night our resident python would slither down one of the corner poles and hunt for mice or frogs beneath the kitchen sink, then by day would curl up in the rafters and sleep. We had no running hot water, so we bathed outside in a cast iron bath with a fire lit beneath it. In the afternoons, we'd spark it up and lie under a dusky sky playing games with the kids, seeing who could spot the first star. Mum and Dad loved this bath and would jump in together and usually end up with a kid or two as well. And while they bathed, they marvelled at the view of trees and mountains and the huge expanse of sky above them.

It was on one of these visits that Dad and I built a rock wall together. We had collected rocks beforehand in preparation. Dad chose the solid base rocks, placing them in practical and aesthetically pleasing positions, then he deftly spread the mortar around them with a delicate trowel that he controlled like a wand. His work was always sharp and clean. He showed me the best way to lay the rocks and together we built a sturdy and beautiful wall in the front room of the house. Some of the rock work in Dad's garden was built with rocks from our mountain place, delivered on our visits, as though we were cross pollinating strata from our place to theirs. We talked about rocks, methods of building, dry walls that lasted lifetimes. If ever I found a smooth round river rock I would think instantly of Dad, and if it had symmetry, I would pick it up, put it in the car and deliver it to him.

◆

When Dad was diagnosed with Parkinson's, he didn't exhibit the uncontrolled tremors that are often associated with the disease, but rather displayed a distinctive shuffle, particularly indoors, as though he couldn't lift his feet to take steps. Outside was a different matter. A keen bushwalker from way back, Dad could suddenly walk in leaps and bounds as though being exposed to the sky and open air freed him. I remember being nervous for him as we planned the Grand Canyon walk in the Blue Mountains, but there was no need. Dad still managed to rock hop with more agility than the rest of us.

It was early on that Dad lost facial expression in a condition called 'hypomimia' giving him a deadpan look, so the eyes are a better indication of how he is feeling. I remember asking him if his eyes were sore one day because they were red. He looked at me as though I'd upset him then boomed, 'His eyes are red as fire with weeping.' This was a favourite line of Dad's from *Julius Caesar*, an onlooker describing Mark Antony after Caesar's death. Dad would talk about Marlon Brando; how brilliant he was as Mark Antony in the film. 'If you ever find a copy, get it for me would you Kate? It's a magnificent film,' he gushed. I was awed by Dad's memory and passion, his love of words and sudden dramatics, still so full of knowledge and language and ideas.

◆

Dad had always been a very affectionate person, tickling or hugging us, chasing us in the surf, mucking around, and he was particularly loving with mum. Often, when we'd walk into the kitchen as kids and later as adults, they'd be wrapped in each other's arms. They both loved a hug. As Dad got older, he became quite emotional and would tear up as he told us stories about his mother or father or about anything that moved him.

Of the many things Dad lost to Parkinson's was his affectionate nature. It wasn't immediate, but happened gradually, as though the emotional part of his brain was slowly being turned off. And, as though Shakespeare's sense of dramatic irony had a cruel hand in it, Dad lost his ability to weep.

In 2018, Dad had a serious fall, hitting his head and causing a brain injury that stopped us all in our tracks.

◆

Standing at the top of the staircase Mum sees Dad fall, only three or four stairs, but he hits his head and lies unconscious. She is frantic. She calls the ambulance, and he is taken to hospital. The family hold vigil at his bedside, hearts clenched. He wakes, pulls at the sheets and his body writhes. Delirium, they tell us. He has had a brain bleed. He pulls the feeding tube from his nose and rips at the canula in his hand. They scan him daily to see the state of his brain and after a week they decide to operate to relieve the pressure. He is eighty-four years old. We sit outside the operating theatre and wait as they drill through dad's skull and drain the pooled blood. We comfort each other that the surgeon knows what he's doing.

Afterwards there is always someone by Dad's side. When it's me I try to get him to talk, I hold his hand, 'Dad, do you know who I am?' I pester until finally he looks at me and answers, 'Kate,' and I am jubilant. 'Why can't I piss properly?' he asks me. This isn't how he usually talks but he has had a catheter in for over a week. I harass the nurses to take it out.

◆

In rehab they restrain Dad in a wheelchair to stop him from trying to walk. He is unsteady and the restraint is for his own good, but he doesn't understand and gets aggressive. The doctor tells us that aggression often occurs after brain injury. They sedate him, and it's heartbreaking. I don't want to leave him. One day he throws himself and his wheelchair on its side. It is a huge cumbersome chair, Dad's strength Herculean. Sometimes he is aggressive with me. He squeezes my hand till it hurts and tells me to go away. I am stricken with grief.

◆

From rehab Dad goes into aged care. He is miserable and angry and frustrated, though, at this stage, he is still able to communicate. He loves the nurses, and sometimes the family can go in for meals with him. The dining room is a circus. The TV is loud and there's music coming from a speaker somewhere. Residents are wandering, one lady, a school teacher from way back is trying to control the classroom telling us all to be quiet. I talk to a man at Dad's table who looks remarkably with it. His name is David, and he tells me about his life in Ireland. I get his life story. The next time I see him I smile and say hello. He looks at me without recognition. 'Remember me, David?' I say, 'I'm Kate, we met the other day.' 'No, I don't,' he says, 'but nice to meet you, Kate.' Dad doesn't seem to notice the dining room chaos, but when I leave him, I am bereft.

◆

Mum is wracked with guilt. Dad wants to come home, but he is so unsteady on his feet, and she doesn't know if she can cope. She is old too. He talks to his children as though he is divorced, as though his wife is at fault for his condition. The family bring him home to visit but when it's time to leave, he refuses and sits on the ground and won't get up. It's devastating to see what life has dealt him.

◆

After a year in aged care and another stint in rehab Mum brings Dad home to live. The house has been fitted out with rails and handles, the bathroom modified, a hospital bed bought, and home help organised. She is nervous, wondering how they'll manage living together again.

Dad is stubborn and becomes more so in the time he spends in the care of Mum. It's hard work for her, but she's proud she can give him back his home and his garden. Covid hits during Dad's time at home and Mum is grateful he is there with her. 'I'm so glad your father's home,' she tells me. 'Imagine being in aged care during all this lockdown. How terrible it must be for those poor families.'

We all visit often and try to help as much as we can so mum can rest or escape for a swim at the beach. She wears herself down with worry and frustration. Dad can be like a wilful child who fights against her every suggestion. Mum says go this way and he goes the other. Sometimes we have to mediate. Often, mum is in tears, and we urge her to go and have a swim while we look after dad. She rushes off and returns rejuvenated, relaxed and grateful.

On my weekend visits we often go to the beach. I drive, Dad sits in the front next to me, and Mum is wriggling around in the back like an excited child talking nonstop, asking questions but not waiting for answers. She can't hear anyway; she's taken her hearing aids out in case she forgets at the beach. I feel like a parent trying to calm the over excited kids.

When we get there Mum jumps out and heads off down to the water. Dad and I take our time, making our way to our bench overlooking the ocean. I get him an ice cream and we watch Mum as she makes her way to the shore. It's as though she barely has the energy to get there without stumbling the last few steps, almost falling into the water. Then we watch as she comes to life. She emerges from that salty brew renewed, moving more freely, her smile wide, as though she's ready for whatever life has to throw at her. She always urges me to go in, 'Go on love, it's wonderful.' And I wander down a little reluctantly, strip off and make my way slowly into the water. She's right, and I'm grateful she encourages me.

We drive home from the beach, excited and talkative, taking in the warmth of the sun through the glass. When we get there, we set up outside in the sun for lunch. Sometimes it feels as though we are part of a comedy skit, Mum and Dad both hard of hearing and I'm the translator passing the message from one to the other. Mum mishears things and takes the conversation in a totally new direction. When she remembers its Friday, she nearly jumps out of her skin, 'Oh love, Costa's on tonight. It's my favourite night if the week.'

◆

As I help Dad to bed that night, I know I should hold these moments close. Dad's giving Gardening Australia praises as he walks down the hall, 'They do a marvellous job, don't they?'

He brushes his teeth and goes to the loo and while he's seated, I help him put his pyjamas on. Then I take his hands in mine and help him walk to his bed, one skinny leg after another. I make sure he sits far enough up the bed, so his feet don't hit the end, then he swings his legs up, his head landing on his tower of pillows as he relaxes. I plump the doona around him, then scratch his head as he closes his eyes, 'That's lovely,' he says. He looks so at ease after the effort and exertion of the day, and I sit and share a peaceful moment with him.

Dad sleeps in the room my sister and I slept in as children, and for a moment I am a child again lying in bed, my sister in the twin bed beside me, and dad, a young man,' standing at the door saying a prayer as he wishes us goodnight.

And forty-five years later, I am putting him to bed, 'Lay me down like a stone, Lord,' I whisper in his ear. 'And raise me up like new bread,' he answers.

◆

At the end of 2019, devastating bushfires destroyed lives, houses and huge areas of land in NSW. Our mountain home was burnt down. We were no longer living there but it was where the kids' lives had begun so it remained a special place to us.

Walking up the hill after the fires was surreal. The bush that had been thick and lush was gone and you could see for miles down valleys and through the pitch blackened trunks of trees that no longer had undergrowth beneath them. When we reached our place, all we could see were crumpled sheets of tin lying on the ground. The mud brick wall had collapsed, but Dad's rock wall remained, the only thing that seemed to have survived the inferno. As the site was cleared, we discovered the fire had weakened the rocks and as soon as there was any movement the rocks began to crumble. The wall Dad and I built was no longer standing. It was devastating, it should have outlived us all.

◆

The last time I saw Dad at home was October 2021. He was standing with Mum and my sister beneath the huge grey gum out the front of the house, waving me off as I headed home. Dad had had another fall during my visit and had broken his shoulder and his elbow. His shoulder was in plaster and held close to his body by a sling, affecting his balance even more than usual and, the morning of my departure, he was attempting to walk without his stick. Mum yelled at him to be careful, still traumatised by this latest fall, and ran off in tears while I tried to explain to him that if he didn't do as mum asked, she wouldn't be able to look after him anymore. He looked at me furiously and yelled, 'I want to go home,' and his words hit me like a thump. 'You are home, dad,' I whispered, taking his hand.

◆

'The problem is they're keeping us alive too long,' Mum laments, as we drive home after visiting Dad in aged care. 'We really need to talk about our funerals,' she says to me, 'I want one of those wicker caskets. Yes, we'll both have wicker caskets. And we want to be buried. Your father's always been against cremation but whatever is best for the environment is what I want,' she says seriously. I find it hard to talk about. The thought of losing Mum is too much to bear. I think she'd be happy to go for a swim and never return, none of this suffering on dry land for her. Just an endless swim and a return to her element.

◆

Dad will be ninety this year and he no longer has the strength to walk, his legs are stiff and constricted like some of the children I used to nurse when I worked in the hospital, their bodies a burden. He still manages to surprise us though. Many times, we've thought the end was near, and he picks up and starts eating and talking again.

He has always been strong willed.

◆

My sister is with Dad, and he is sleeping soundly. When he opens his eyes, she asks, 'Did you have a nice sleep?' 'Very nice,' he answers, 'I didn't know which train to catch.' Then he closes his eyes and falls asleep again. Dad caught trains to school as a boy in Sydney and often talked of his childhood in Oatley and I wonder, when he said he wanted to go home, the morning of his argument with mum, if he was thinking of his childhood home.

It's a mystery how the ageing mind works, how it can return to childhood with such clarity, leaving the present and near past, foggy and vague. As though more recent memories are being shed in order to uncover the place we began.

◆

Dad and I are outside in the sun. I push him in his chair around the garden looking at the Gymea lily almost ready to bloom. I ask the nurse if I can stay and give Dad his lunch, and I set up a table in the sun. Before we know it, cloud has gathered, and it starts to rain. I wheel Dad up under the shelter of the verandah and as I feed him his lunch, we witness a massive downpour. The rain pelts down in sheets and Dad's eyes light up. 'Boy, it's heavy,' I say, and Dad looks awestruck as though this is the most exciting thing he's seen in a long time. 'It's good,' he answers, eyes gleaming, the way they did when he'd show us his beloved wattle in full bloom, and I am struck by his ability to still find delight in the world.

Afterwards I take him upstairs to his room and he is exhausted. I help him lie down in bed and as his head hits the pillow, he sighs, and he is out to it. I take off his shoes and put a blanket over him and as I lean down and kiss his forehead, I feel like a mother putting her child to bed.

Rain is still teeming down, the wind swirling in gusts as I run to the car. I fumble at the door; I can't get the key in the lock, water dripping down my face, I get the key in, turn it and I jump in, drenched. I lay my head against the steering wheel and crumple. It doesn't get any easier leaving him here.

The rain eases and I smile as I think of Dad's delight in the storm today. The Moreton Bay fig tree is glowing, and in a day or two the red trumpets of the Gymea lily will push their way open towards the sky.

Kate Giles began her working life as a nurse. She now works in education at a primary school on Dunghutti country on the mid-north coast of NSW while studying creative writing through Macquarie University. She writes poetry, short stories and fragments. When her father became ill in 2018, she began writing about him.

ME/CFS AND ME

Melanie Ifield

I

A (very) unscientific Abstract

This is a story about living with a chronic long-term illness called Myalgic Encephalomyelitis (ME), most commonly known as Chronic Fatigue Syndrome (CFS), or the combination—ME/CFS.

No one who has ME/CFS experiences it in the same way.

Some have it so mildly they can work a few days a week, though they may get home after work and go straight to bed, relying on loved ones to get dinner and help them shower. You don't see that.

Others never go back to work again.

Some spend days on the couch, hoarding the energy to shower and feed themselves, like dragons with gold. Others lie in darkened rooms, never to see the outside of their four walls again. You *really* don't see that.

Symptoms include:

Insomnia—with one or two hours sleep a night—or the direct opposite, sleeping up to twenty hours per day; extreme exhaustion (no matter how much you sleep); joint inflammation/pain; bloating; headaches; migraine; brain fog; cognitive dysfunction; blurred vision; light sensitivity; auditory sensitivity; sensitivity to touch (ie actual pain when being touched); slurred speech; chemical sensitivity; food sensitivity; digestive dysfunction; elimination dysfunction; IBS; difficulty swallowing; light-headedness; faintness; blackouts; pooling of blood in extremities/abdomen; dysautonomia (for example, Postural Orthostatic Tachycardia Syndrome—POTS); inability to walk far; inability to walk at all; muscle weakness; post exertional malaise (PEM); sensory overload; chronic diarrhoea and/or constipation; being couch bound; being bedbound; being housebound; heart palpitations/tachycardia; dizziness; nausea; inability to regulate body temperature (including sensitivity to changes in external temperature); chest pain; shortness of breath; low blood pressure; chronic localised or conversely, generalised pain; complete and total collapse leading to hospitalisation.

There are no broadly effective medical treatments for this condition, and due to the increased sensitivity to any/all chemicals, and every person's body being completely different, many drugs to alleviate symptoms simply create untenable side effects. Some are rejected wholesale by the body. Recovery from ME/CFS is estimated to be less than 7%; while 25% are totally bedbound in varying stages of darkened rooms, with no sound, and rarely any human touch. In between those two extremes, the vast majority drift in a sliding scale of physical and mental abilities, left to find a life for themselves, calling themselves the #millionsmissing, as they drop out of their previous lives and simply...disappear.

II

The Art of Illness

A long time ago, in a moment of 'compassion' from someone, I was told that suffering is something I am doing to myself. Some meditation gurus and others (I'm not sure anymore, it was a long time ago and the cognitive dysfunction and brain fog have wiped out smaller moments in my life) believe that suffering is simply longing for what isn't. They also state that life just *is*—we just exist. What is happening in our lives is what it is, and it is the longing for what it *isn't*, that creates the suffering.

I took that onboard. Sort of. At the time. I thought, okay, acceptance! That's something all those gurus speak of. Acceptance is a surrendering that brings you to the point where you can say the liberating words 'it is what it is'. Joy—or if not that, then at least an approximation! Without the inner longing for something that isn't, and may never be again, the suffering will disappear. I could get behind something like that! No suffering.

Perhaps, I stripped this concept of acceptance down too far and missed some vital bits. If this seems to diminish something you have held close to your heart, or offends those of you who believe in such a thing, well, Welcome to my world. Too many people casually offend the chronically ill 'me' in their need to make me feel better, or at least, make my life more acceptable to them.

Acceptance and surrender actually don't change pain, anyway. Not the mammoth, screaming into the pillow, 'give me the good drugs and don't stint on them please', kind of pain. The pain where you throw up for hours, where you lie on that narrow little hospital bed, drenched in sweat with heat radiating off you as the animal within you, unaffected by eons of civilisation, is too distressed to regulate temperature. The kind of pain where, after enduring this for some time, the body starts to shake; it has gone through enough, it is heading into shock, trembling, with rigors that make the metal frame of that hospital bed rattle. Where the drugs dripping into tiny veins seem to take forever to reach the dimmer switch. Where exhaustion hits you like the proverbial truck running you over, and lifting your arm is a step too far, so you are handfed, even in your thirties and forties, because, you know, humiliation isn't something they warn you about when you get sick.

The loss of ability to do the smallest thing for myself at some stages of this journey have crushed my independent spirit and led to some of the lowest moments of my life. Unless you experience the soul destroying need to have your parents spoon feed you or hold you up over a bucket while you pee, as you simply cannot walk to the bathroom, you can't begin to imagine the skin crawling humiliation that comes with complete physical failure in the prime of your life.

The brain isn't really active in those moments. It isn't activity thinking—oh I long to be somewhere or someone else. It is just becoming—pain. Shit, more pain. Here comes some more. How many nerve endings can we fry? The suffering is coming from *pain*. From overload and distress. The primitive animal has taken over and it whimpers, and it squirms and yes, it probably wants to crawl away, or out of its own skin. But there isn't really any *longing*, per se, as thinking has left the building. Except perhaps a longing for death. So maybe they're right about the idea of suffering being the gap between what is and what you want it to be; but then again maybe they're wrong.

Suffering can just be that. Suffering. In the moment. The pain of the moment can be of the flesh, not an existential crisis of longing to be elsewhere. Simply the basic suffering of any animal left too long at some point way beyond their endurance. If you break a bone, or give birth, there is an expectation that the pain will fade, that time will go on and things will heal and change. With long term, chronic illness where symptoms come and go—forever—there is no end. There just is moment by moment fluctuations of degrees of Hell.

This got me thinking about *degrees* of things. Well, yes, degrees of suffering but also, degrees of bodily *failure*.

When I first became ill, I was stuck like a pincushion, every test under the sun performed using my rather nice and thin red blood. The low blood pressure just making it all that more exciting when they took seven or nine vials of the good stuff from the veins that liked to hide so much, that people have been known to have to go in with that pointy needle more than once, digging around to find a line that would cough up the liquid. That is always a joy.

I was tested for everything, including Addison's Disease, which, if you Google it, is 'adrenal insufficiency'. Where those pesky little buggers don't produce the right amounts of the pep-you-up juice. I didn't have that. Seems my markers were in the 'you'll be fine' range. Which brings me back to the *degrees* of things.

See, where do those markers start and stop? Who says that, out of 100—where 0 is you are *so* screwed, and 100 is you'll be climbing Mt

Everest any day now—let's pluck a random number, 20!—who says that if you are over 20, you'll be fine and if you are under, we'll help you with the drugs and more investigation and the whole medical world will work hard on your behalf and we'll get your life back for you? What happens to those who are only 21 on this scale?

What happens when—shock, gasp, horror—you don't actually rate on any test? When there *is* no test for your particular illness? You can't hold up a shiny report card that says 'you failed, you have xyz'; your experience of illness, or alarming symptomology, is negated, is undiagnosable and thus a mystery, so you are medically shunned, rather than helped?

Welcome to the Thunderdome.

III

"Not to be healthy... is one of the few sins
that modern society is willing to recognise and condemn."
Robertson Davies, The Cunning Man (1994)
Quoted in: Collins Gem Quotations1997 p.209

Medical models

For many who are experiencing chronic illness, the stigma attached by society leaves them stranded. They are no longer in the 'in' club of healthy people going about what is considered a 'normal' life and yet, they still exist. We all know what society can do to those who don't fit in. More so now, it seems, with social media, than at any other time in history. Healthy people can 'well-splain' illness to those who don't look ill enough, or look to sick. Or quite sick, or who are sick 'too long'. The stigma around having to be on disability pension, or any sort of governmental help when you look 'perfectly okay or normal' (whatever that is), leaches deep into the soul. The judging stare and disbelief of strangers. The pitiless condemnation from successive governments about 'welfare cheats' that makes you feel less than human having to rely on welfare. And the endless contempt of a society that feels that, somehow, some people deserve their fate.

While *not* being healthy is fast becoming a growth industry in a cliquey kind of way (just look at all the blogs and places you can get all kinds of information to help yourself—anyone for Goop?), society hasn't changed the wellness goalposts, leaving those experiencing life outside feeling lost and alone. Throw in an illness that is so complex, affects virtually every system within the body and plays merry hell with virtually every organ, and then not only does society vilify sufferers, but the medical professional does too.

Many years ago, when I was young, I heard about a condition called 'chronic fatigue' which was laughingly called 'yuppie flu'. The terrible thing about developing this 'yuppie flu', now termed Myalgic Encephalomyelitis/Chronic Fatigue Syndrome (ME/CFS), is that it is so random, targeting anyone, any age. And the medical profession doesn't seem to know much about it. It doesn't even get its own cool 'disease' label, just a syndrome. A collection, if you will, of symptoms that are thrown in the 'too hard basket'. Add in Postural Orthostatic Tachycardia Syndrome (POTS), (another group of symptoms affecting blood pressure) just for fun, swirl them both around within the autonomic nervous system and suddenly the patient (me) is being told take an antidepressant and learn to live with it.

If you can (added under the breath by me).

Then I did manage to meet a doctor who believed; who can't offer traditional help, but by acknowledging the issues this illness gives me, the patient, actually offered me something just as good: *belief*.

Coping alone

The stigma around illness, around the sheer bad luck of it all, can close in and people are abandoned because no one wants to share their fate. What if their bad luck rubs off on me? What if I get sick too? And... the eternal sympathy fatigue of, *Aren't you better yet?*

I don't blame anyone for those thoughts and fears. When I was healthy and strong, I had no time for the weak and the ill. I too, didn't like the idea of lightning striking twice and hitting me. And always asking someone how they are feeling only to receive the same 'terrible, how are you?' must get pretty wearying. I know it does from the perspective of having to keep saying it.

Somewhere along this journey, though, I started to realise that perhaps the person who told me that in life our suffering is self-created, wasn't actually being mean. It was an *offering*. A chance for self-determination and a chance for taking back some control of my life. For if, in actual fact, suffering was simply the gap between what my life is and what I wished with all my heart it could be/was, then by eliminating that gap, I could get a handle on things—*for myself.*

Long-term chronic illness steals into your life insidiously and pries all the things you loved out of your grasp. The future is no longer full of potentials, friends and family or even a job with superannuation. There is no super, no money for 'extras' and holidays overseas, to the beach or to anywhere, really. When I curl up into a little ball, knees to my chin, heels under my butt and vomit my stomach contents up for a few hours until there isn't even any bile, I wonder—what will become of me if I am like this at sixty? Or seventy? Will I be able to curl up around my agony? Or will the looming osteoporosis (lack of dairy—body won't tolerate it—added to no weight bearing exercise equals poor bones) have me snapping myself in two? Who will hold me up when I literally fall over and who will clean up when I can't make the toilet? Will I be dependent on paid help? How will I pay for this and will they care enough to massage painful joints with Deep Heat and tuck the sheets in around my shoulders when I can't lift my arms?

IV

One day

(Now I'm no longer bedridden)

Today I woke up at 4.30am. Again. But at least I had been asleep. I have moved my bed so it lies lengthwise to the window so I can watch the sky. There are two particular stars in my slice of sky that I talk to late at night and as I wait for the coming dawn. They keep me company from 4am until I either doze back off, or until the rotation of the coming day slides them beyond my sight. They flash as the shrub outside the window bends, buckling in the breeze; now I see them, now I don't. They're company. Of sorts.

By the time the grey light of dawn washes out the remaining stars, my head is heavy and my heart is pounding. Soon, all too soon, I will have to get up. I place a blackout mask on my eyes to shield them from the glare of the sun. The light filtering through and around the corners of the mask makes me wince. The transition from dark to light can be traumatic, light lancing my ultra-sensitive optic nerve, making it freak out with running eyes, pain, and headaches. The mask eases it somewhat. My body doesn't like surprises, even ones that sneak up slowly every day. Light hurts, sharp noises hurt, and the expectations that come with a new day make me tired before I even get out of bed.

I lift the corner of my mask and let some light in. This slow introduction tells my body, 'Hey, this is what's happening. We are about to see daylight. Get used to the idea!' But each time I remove the mask, I flinch and my eyes want to hide. If I lie there and let myself relax, eventually, I am ready for the next stage. I sit up.

I am in my forties, but I move with the studied care of someone in their eighties. I should know, I live with my parents who are in their eighties. They took me in twelve years ago when I could no longer look after myself. We have aged together, marinating in the harsh realities of the elderly and infirm. If you don't laugh, you cry.

I have clothes in a pile less than a metre from the bed. I no longer have a permanent vomit bucket beside my bed, as I have finally reached a point where I don't randomly vomit when my body is having a bad day. This is progress. Though I do carry a hospital issue vomit bag in my handbag, in my car, my parent's car and my mother's handbag. No point in tempting fate.

Even so, I don't think I suffer from malnutrition these days. This, too, is progress. My nice slow morning routine was developed to avoid the morning nausea.

Finally, I make it out of my room.

My head feels thick and woolly, my bones ache, my back burns down each knob of the spine and my eyes are gritty. A wash with cold water and I am ready for breakfast.

I chat with my parents as they eat toast and porridge. I can smell the Vegemite and wish I could eat that too. I used to love Vegemite, or creamed honey, on fresh soft bread. What a treat that would be! But it is hard to find bread I can eat, even these days of gluten-free and organically sourced ingredients.

It is ten o'clock by the time I get a mug of green tea and walk into the room I use as a study/lounge. There is an electric chair in here; with a touch of a button it lifts me up and out or lowers me down and raises a footrest. The best investment. Across from that is a wide screen TV.

With the red lensed glasses, I can watch a screen for a few hours. But I must take into account combining the phone, with the laptop and TV, so I eke out what I use and for how long. If I play fast and loose with the rules my body retaliates with headaches, burning eyes, buzzing legs and insomnia. Like I need more insomnia in my life.

I am trying to muster up the energy and mental capacity to do some writing. Some time ago, I called myself a writer. But a writer, or author, needs to write. My brain is stuck in a fog and the strength needed to marshal the troops into some sort of focus is beyond me today. Today, I binge old TV shows for my allotted time. They are popcorn for the brain, allowing me to be entertained without actually having to think. There are no surprises watching something I've seen before. Can't watch anything suspenseful, or the heartrate gets out of control and takes hours to settle back down again, wiping out energy and mental capacity in one plunge. So, steady as she goes.

I eat a little lunch, and rest. I turn the laptop on and check my emails. This makes me feel connected to the world and allows me the chance to feel productive. Today is not a good day and writing will have to wait.

By late afternoon I am shaky, my stomach churning over lunch (God help me, stomach, I have restricted my diet as far as I can! What will you accept without too much whinging?) and my legs feeling a little like spaghetti. It's the internal shakes that are of most concern. They make my muscles weak and my head spin a little. I haven't seen anyone except my parents for days now, and I would love to go into town and see a friend, but not today. When the adrenals kick in to give me a lift in the energy part of the program, they can stay in a state of 'hyped-up' for hours and leave me feeling buzzed and jabbering at full speed. If you meet me and I'm talking a million miles too fast and laughing like a hyena, then my adrenals are spiking and once they are done...I'll hit rock bottom and collapse. Beware.

Going out of the house, for any reason, takes effort, compromise and determination. It requires the sort of preparation I imagine that goes into any campaign strategy. I determine if I really wish to attend (well, I always *really* wish to attend, but I have to compromise); how much time I can afford to spend out with people without ending up bedridden or in hospital; I rest all the day before and the day of, only expending the minimal amount of energy; I line up hydration, pain meds, support and make the most of every second of freedom. I have also made sure that I have not planned anything else for the days after. So, if I say to you, sorry I can't make it, it doesn't mean you are not of value. It means I used that 'outside' energy in the last day or so and I am hibernating until the pain and exhaustion recedes. Mostly, it's very, very rarely that I go out.

It's been 14 years since ME/CFS first entered my life, but grief can hit you at any time. It is cyclical, I have been told. One minute you are accepting and living the best life you can, given the circumstances; the next you are torn up inside, grief raking your soul. You don't ever become accustomed to life without yourself. The heartbreak as muscle groups shrink and fascia tissues harden into old leather. The yoga, the Tai Chi, the flexibility—all gone.

I love that my friends can share their lives with me. I love that they are comfortable enough to phone me if something wonderful happens. This is joy! I am so happy for them. Mostly. Sometimes, though, the loss of not being able to travel, or play squash, or go to a party, or a friend's wedding. The weeping wound of all the versions of me that have disappeared.. It is not their fault. And it is not mine.

V

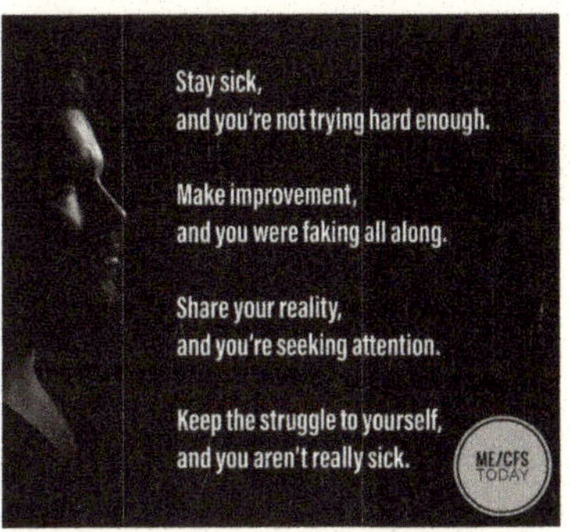

Shared By @millionsmissingvoice on Instagram/Facebook
Reposted on Facebook in the ME/CFS Australia group

This post was recently reshared on Facebook (May 2022) and it made me think. Long term, chronic, invisible illness is a trap. Not just the obvious one—where people fall into the hole of illness, get lost and never escape. But the not-so-obvious one, where people are full of advice but little understanding, and run out of patience, getting that wonderful old 'sympathy-fatigue'.

I have been told to gain weight, lose weight, eat meat/go vegan, do more exercise/rest more, do yoga/Pilates/aquatherapy...the list feels endless. If I am silent and just let the person explain to me how their suggestions would instantly make me feel better if I could just be more motivated, then they feel like they've cured me themselves. If I am seen as resistant to help, or if I don't attempt one or all fifty-five of their cures, then I am clearly not trying and obviously want to remain ill. The trap within the trap.

The fact I am not giving your suggestion the good old college try isn't because I don't want to get better, or think you're full of shit (though, depending on how ridiculous the idea is, I just might). It is because I've tried it. So please-stop-telling-me-to-exercise-more-before-I-stab-myself (or you) with a spoon.

I became disabled through an illness. I wasn't born this way, and I am still finding my way. As I age and as my carers age, the future feels unstable and a little frightening. Of course, there have been, and still are, deep, dark moments where the pain, the muscle weaknesses—the sheer inability—caused/s me to drown in tears.

But that isn't to say there isn't hope. Because there is. I have gone from totally bedridden and unable to feed myself, to learning to walk again and sitting up unsupported. Some days I do just that bit more. This is not only progress: it is a blessing. It is hope.

Always.

All ways.

Melanie Ifield .Melanie is the author of seven novels and several short stories. Her short fiction, *Jessica Saves the Day*, won the 2004 Nairda Lynne Award writing for 8–12-year-olds, and her adult short story, The Lonely House, won first place in a 2022 writing competition, subsequently published in the women's magazine *Mona*. In 2022, Melanie graduated with a Master of Creative Writing from Macquarie University, earning the Macquarie University Award for Academic Excellence. Her short stories have also been published in and read on *Antipodean SF journal* and radio, and in *Specul8* anthologies.

Bodies of Water

Elizabeth Walton

You will not see the adjustments I make stepping out in shallow gait. The pivot of the ankle to match the grade of the slope, the internal rotation of the hip, the slow pace with faster strides to keep up, to walk as I do. Slower when cold, faster on warmth.

You will not see my foot at an odd angle, sliding my guitar case under the bed. My finger tendons softly slipping the joints that knuckle down a C note, or a D, snapping sound into place. Knuckles no longer capable of pressing soft nylon strings or sitting at a piano to press down black and white keys. Pressing down instead the soft glass on the phone to stream Andres Segovia's Reveries, which my own hands no longer play.

Look out to sea, you can see me any day, slipping softly into the flow, craving water as my cure the way Charles Darwin did. Floating his hopes for voyages, for discovery. So many ships slipping by if water had not pulled him back into the flow.

I didn't know when I was young that things just slip by. I've never had that kind of thinking. In my high school years, I thought I'd play music forever, as I waited beneath the shelter in my green uniform of a boarded-up shop. Leaning into my black guitar case.

My friend Keith and I caught the bus to our guitar lessons straight from school. On Thursday afternoons we arrived at Nena Beretin's studio, hungry for potato scallops. But we respected the studio lined with posters of André Segovia, and didn't want to bring in the smell of overheated oil. So, we dipped out of fast food indulgences.

Our music slid out of sound boxes as we played, then Nena would take us back to the start, the sound gliding under the door and down the Lino stairs, spilling into the street.

Sound from a different place, an older time.

Nena drew the music of Andalusia down the back streets of Sydney, guitar strings, tremolo, the rasgueado of our right-hand sweeps. Ambitious exercises flowed past the film camera shop, the Dinkum Donuts, the old barber with the red and blue poles, GJ Coles. The surging entrance to Westfield.

Movement was economical then, the small adjustment of a finger on a string. Now, movement is key again, though movement will never be what it was.

I can go on forever walking along a flat path, once I'm going. It's the hills that water me down, making swish of softening ligaments, but you will not see the micro steps I take to keep the ankle from lilting, the toe from dislocating. The mutiny of choices I make when chewing bread to avoid disrupting the jaw. You will not see the many ways I overcompensate. Adjusting to circumstance. Swimming to the conditions.

It was a Wednesday, the day I awoke to new tissue trouble.

Tendon and muscle rupture; the dislocations. All of that I am used to. But this was different.

This was to awaken as a fish with no fins, my body a mass without active limbs to move me out of bed. My legs splayed in curly brackets that held the trickster words: and now we move feet to the *floor, and now we stand, we put the body upright and breathe*.

There would be no making of any bed, no ground control to land my sleep-filled feet, not even the weakest signal to bring them over side of the bed. All communication was thrown; neural pathways, lost. Richard had to help, lifting and placing each free pivoting hip, mindful of the wincing, the dreadful murmur, the sense of life as it had been known in times when I couldn't walk or sit or run or stand for long returning.

By end of day things had improved. I could walk with a rope to saddle my foot, lifting my leg by hand.

Even the rope had a history—a past life of retting and stripping, spinning and twisting. Rope had become a life source that disambiguated ordinary movement. The loops of twining jute rubbed the soft skin of my hand, but this new movement was more economical, more careful than using the crutches we picked up at the chemist shop opposite the pool.

Inside that chemist, we were kids stealing a hit, only there were no drugs; our thrill was the sound of adjusting the slots of one-size-only supports, the satisfying ping as the pins slotted in. Even now, the crutches are by my desk, next to the rope, near my classical guitar and two pianos. Claiming contested space, leaning against the cupboard door, for those days when I can't stand.

Everything finds a way to slot in. Guitars and pianos in want of a song. A hip in want of a rope. A body in want of water, if only to swim and float.

The whole body is water. Connective tissue, around 80 percent. Skin, a little less, the heart a little more. My body sometimes works. Other times I return to my state as a fish that has no fins. A fish in want of water.

Everything was fine until that day when it wasn't. Until I got out of bed, slowly to avoid the spins, only to find I could not stand. I could not walk. Slowly crawling, getting stuck halfway. Calling out to Richard and he didn't hear. There'd been no pain the week before.

◆

'You'll want a hip replacement,' the GP says. The physio says; the chiro says. They all say the same. A hip that sat me through countless piano and guitar performances needed to be cut out and turfed.

Both life and limb were at a loose end.

Scans proved nothing other than inflammation, which resolved over time, and then the medical industry moved on as though nothing happened.

We have done the rounds, since then, Richard driving when I cannot. Tossing the crutches in back with the dog, visiting a dowdy brown brick building overlooking the sea, where I start at the pool.

I take out my black Mastercard to pay for the membership, I slide it back beside my collection of driving licenses from other years, when other unexplained injuries required other memberships. Visits to other pools.

Like Charles Darwin, taking the waters was always my cure. The bands of tissue connecting my feet that are stressed and rigid where they are not torn. A subluxation in the neck making it hard to swallow. The water promised to release the prism of pain that had me trapped.

On those swimming days, life was good; those days were enough. Those days made life a Partita, a Ronsard, a Romance de los Pinos; they made breathing space between the movements, each day a dance, each gigue something new. But by the time I could handle a ten-lap routine I was benched by something else. Calf tears made it impossible to walk. Every week I added a new challenge to the list, a day, now and then, in between.

In my 20s, I did a whole degree standing up and lying down flat, my supervisor passing exam booklets down. It's only been bad again since the fish-with-no-fin moment. Then it was good, then not so good.

I still can't sit for long, so standing it is. Standing at my desk, I shift my weight, one foot to the other. Check the minutes, eight, nine.

Ten minutes typing, then spin down the hall, trying not to catch my shoe in the loose brown threads the dog has scuffed, racing up and down, excited for a walk, a meal, a visit outside to the sun; none of which I can provide.

In the pool, the body is transformed. I glide through a shimmer of hope that my shoulder isn't poorly aligned. Sculpting water, each palm, touching down, the morning sun gliding through the winter window. The rainbow of prisms, a *Dark Side of The Moon* below the lane.

Between the creams, machines. Heat packs. Dips in the sea for the ice thrill. In the warm buoyancy of neutral gravity, my body seems to work quite well. But I can't move very far outside of the pool. Nor can I live in the pool.

On Saturday night, I prop in front of the TV. See a woman in finery and Queen Victoria braids, a woman reminiscent of Holly Hunter in Jane Campion's film, *The Piano*. Women who fit inside the bodice of a certain world, pinned to the mercy of men.

Hip jamming on the couch, I sit for longer than I should, long enough to see Charles Darwin, the father of evolutionary thinking in John Collee's film, *Creation*. His wife, Emma Wedgwood closing the lid on her wooden piano. Taking her foot off the sustain pedal to walk outside and see her husband off in a wooden carriage. She was pregnant and powerless to protest. So she watched the godfather of evolutionary thinking, caught between the hypothesis of the conventional doctor and the experimental treatments at the Water Cure Establishment, where Darwin is told his malaise will not lift until there is a shift in his thinking.

On our way to the gig in the morning, Richard and I are still thinking about Darwin. In other years, Richard lugged all 88 black-and-white keys of my Yamaha into the back of the car. On stage, he clicked my piano stand together.

It's easier to lug a guitar around, but my soft fingers won't work the frets, so keys it is. Or was, until I could no longer sit for a gig. I am the spectator now. Singing harmonies from the sidelines, staying in the audience as long as I can. Movement, as always, is key.

At school, Nena sculpted our guitarist's nails and taught us to move from first position to second position. She called it 'economical', getting from here to there using the least amount of movement possible. Movement for me is no longer about fine motor skills; it's about moving as much as possible in large freestyle swings: the push, the pull, the lift, the lunge, the kick, the hinge.

Sunglasses and beanie on, mid-winter scarf tucked inside an old puffer. Leaving Richard crooning into the mic, I take off, walking behind swelling banks of wattle sculpted to a low hedge by the relentless sea. Back clicking and cracking I walk. Wary of ankles rolling. Rolling away like the sea, like my idea of escaping to a magical island where me and my body might live, pain-free.

◆

People in pain are alive. Alive inside real bodies. Even if they don't talk about it. It's a personal choice to be seen as more than the sum of my sinews, soft and gliding. Not to live every moment through a composition of soft tissue disease. Connective tissue that won't function properly. Causing joint instability, and other strange markers that trace the story of certain genetic conditions. Systemic issues like hypermobile Ehlers-Danlos Syndrome (hEDS), a genetic connective tissue disorder that waters down collagen, the protein that provides strength and elasticity to tissues.

◆

Three months after my fish-with-no-fins moment, I ditch the crutches, hang the rope that lifted my leg on the wall. My hips walk again, but my calf muscles constantly tear. I adjust my laps to reduce kick pressure, wear a compression cuff in the water.

Then comes sleeping on the floor for three months.

Then come the headaches from the floor.

I visit the physio every Monday for six weeks. I ask for strengthening exercises—plantar fascia, gastrocnemius, the hips and sacroiliac joints, the neck, the jaw. All the broken, stressed and strained things, the misaligned things. I copy lists into my diary, making stick-man diagrams, borrowing $660 for the visits on my black Mastercard.

The young physio in the black ironed trousers blinks as he tries to release my clicky jaw. And I spend the next six months ignoring the disconnect between jaw and mouth whenever I eat soft things, like lettuce. White bread.

◆

Like writing, music is an endurance game, not the short fast sprint, but people didn't talk about athletic fitness for musos when I was a kid. There was no talk of the strength required to sit at a piano for hours every day, or practice Segovia's methods of classical guitar. Like many creatives, practising damaged my vessels, my muscles, my joints. By the age of 30, all those years of practice are written in the body, like a large full stop.

The more creatives write and draw and paint and practice our scales, the more we need to dance, to walk. Get up and move around. I know that now. Life has become all about that. Everything revolves around movement and water.

On a good day, I go out to the garden. In my breakthrough moment, I collect compost buckets Rich has placed in rows, soaked in a glug of water. Gelatinous. Soft like my joints, but it is the weeding that does me in. Just a half hour. Then I have to stop. For two long weeks I can barely walk.

I force myself to the pool. The brick wall collects a shadow of me that grows larger with every flare, every episode. Every ripped meniscus, every hip displacement that sends me indoors, trying not to cough or sneeze for fear of damage.

Things are different in the water. Buoyancy does what my body will not. I now have the strength for 20 laps, even at the height of a flare. Afterwards, I hand over my wrists while pathologists try to extract secrets from my hard-to-find-veins, searching for genetic conditions like hypermobility spectrum and connective tissue disorders like Ehlers-Danlos Syndrome. Six months of daily exercise prescribed by the physio produces little if any result.

'Rest,' Richard reminds me on the phone. 'Use the cream, use the massage machine.'

The wheat bag is heated in the oven, next to the chilli paste I baked in an open tray, no chopping required. Life goes on. With you. Without you. And chopping strains the wrists.

At the pool, I follow the black line up the lane, squeegeed under the water over last year's patches of paint. Patched like the hob of the steaming shower in the cold change rooms, where the bright mound at the edge of the stall is painted eggs easy over. It's painted over last year's patches, which are now watered down to canary yellow. A winged warning in a cage; watery like my ligaments. Like so many lemons bathed in salt; it softens into something else. I avoid the neurological chiropractors who tell me, like Charles Darwin, that malaise is mostly in the mind. To heal, requires changing modes of thinking, they say.

Messages from the tissues to the brain. Processes of the normal feedback loop tell the body where it is in space and time. These things are tricky for people living with genetic conditions which impact the way the ear processes information through the vestibular mechanisms, as happens with Ehlers-Danlos syndrome. Dizziness, balance problems, and vertigo.

◆

'Can you touch your toes?' my GP asks. Always so supportive. Unlike my watery body.

Bending over, I place my palms beneath my feet.

'It's Ehlers-Danlos syndrome. EDS,' she says. 'That's definitely what's going on.'

Though the condition is well researched, it is little understood. The blurred eyesight, the unusual response to drugs, and, of course, the hypermobile joints and hints of weirder things like mast cell activation.

'Of course, there is no cure. That much is known,' she says, sounding positive.

◆

The sound of pianos, the sounds of guitar. Segovia's guitar methods, which we studied back in high school, were a challenge for hypermobile joints. Seated in a rigid position with my left foot elevated on a metal footstool, I spent hours each day, looking down at my left hand. The human ear is soothed by the sound of music reflecting on water as smooth as glass.

In 1976, Andres Segovia returned to the place where he played guitar as a child. In Andalusia, he performed seated by an 'estanque'. A body of water with a surface so smooth that it was almost an extension of the polished timber of his guitar.

The sculpted shape of his nail, the smooth water, every sheen condensed the sound, producing a rounder, clearer tone. I was a teenager when I became enchanted by the vision of Segovia, seated by the floodlit pond at the Alhambra Palace, playing Catalan folk songs. He used the water as a glass resonator, creating acoustic impedance between the water and the palace, the air.

Segovia's music flowed into the valley of roses and oranges planted by the Moors during the Nasrid dynasty. The music composed by Albeniz floating around the valley. Gliding as smoothly as a body that can walk without crutches or ropes. The white marble and rammed earth surrounding the *Court of the Myrtles* reflected the mellow timbre of his guitar.

Water as instrument.

◆

I remember Segovia as the water soothes me, like the water that softened Charles Darwin's pain. The lane markers are easy to read. The black bunting flag that marks halfway. Like a piano with the notes drawn on—the C note, the D. It's as easy to read as a guitar dotted in nail polish to show where the fingers are placed. As easy to read as genetic code that flags collagen defects. Genetic mutations that cause hypermobility and mast cell activation, a condition where the body becomes hyperresponsive, fighting wars long after the threat has passed. Asthma wars, allergen wars that keep the body stuck in a cycle of responding. Though not all forms of EDS are as yet discoverable in DNA chains.

Connective tissue disorders are rare. General practitioners can do little to help but print the paperwork.

◆

Referrals, prescriptions.

Apoyando, tirando.

The player performing a tango between the body and the guitar. Each week my friend Keith sat facing each other for two hours while Nena sculpted us. The metacarpal holding the pressure, gently resting one finger on each string, as she leaned in. Only then could we begin. A Sarabande, a Bourrée. Lagrima, my thumb soon collapsing, incapable of the circular movement. For all her sculpting, my nails were gossamer. Too thin to hold their shape.

Collagen proteins strengthen and elasticise the skin, nails, joints, and blood vessels. Cartilage that refuses to hold; the pressure of the joint pain on my thumb too much for the weight of carrying dishes down from the shelf. The pens my fingers won't hold. So much of ordinary life leaning on a thumb.

On a winter morning, I pull myself out of bed, throw on my StingRay one-piece, eating fruit while Richard drives. At the end of the lane, I strip down, plug my ears, and breathe in the chlorine, despite the asthma. I hit the water, bubbles to skin, the sun bowing through the glass. The water on the bay as smooth as Alhambra Palace.

In the water, I reach up to the dive block, lane 'six' marked in black between my elbows, and let the weight of my body drag. Making traction. Making breathing space, for vertebrae and soft discs. Inventing exercises for the thoracic spine that reverse the click in my neck. The soft parts that crumble into shapes a back shouldn't know. Shapes that send ripples of pain down my arms.

I swim at a pace. A powerhouse, a storm of hoping, correcting. Risking the pull if the shoulder is not aligned, not in the right place to plough a body with fins through water.

Like Darwin and Segovia, water is my salve, my resonant surface. It is my analgesic.

I take my split cells of hydrogen and oxygen. Close the books on medical inquiry and return to the water. Water is my goddess now.

Elizabeth Walton received a 2023 Macquarie University Award for Academic Excellence in her Masters of Creative Writing and recently submitted her Master of Research. She commenced her PhD in Creative Writing in 2025. Recent works: *Poetry D'Amour* anthology, *Furphy* prize anthology, longlisted in the Tom Collins Poetry Prize, Creatrix 66, Ros Spencer Poetry Anthology, *Meniscus, Swamp, Overland, Guardian, ABC, Artshub*. Elizabeth received the Anne Edgeworth fellowship in 2022 and was second place in the 2022 AAWP and Woollahra Digital Literary awards.

A Poem About Dad

Lucy Marinelli

Over thirty years ago, I wrote my first poem. I was fifteen. I see it clearly on the single sheet of lined paper, torn from my English book, one of two poems written for year eleven English class. I no longer have a copy, although it's possible it exists tucked away in old papers somewhere. A poem about my dad...

◆

My father turned eighteen on September 10, 1960. In July of 1961, he arrived in Australia after a month at sea. He and his mother, my *Nonna*, were met by his father, who had arrived six years before, and his brother, Michele (Mick), who had travelled over with a couple of friends nine and half years earlier. The reunited family drove from the docks of Melbourne to their new home in the suburbs of Adelaide.

Zio Mick left Italy in 1951 on an adventure with his two best mates — he liked to tell the story of getting a job driving trucks and one night parking, unknowingly, on the tram tracks at Sydney's North Bondi, sleeping in the cabin, only to wake up to find they'd blocked the morning trams. One way or the other, my grandfather and uncle were well-settled by the time my father — *Tonino,* little Toni — and his mum, followed.

The story my dad told is they had to come to Australia, leaving their village Silvi Marina on Italy's Adriatic coast, after his sister's wedding. Apparently, Zia Lina's wedding was so big, it turned the family poor. I knew my aunt as kind and generous, and a formidable woman, never once letting me go for a walk by myself when I visited as a teenager.

◆

The year my father turned 18, 1960, was also the year Mark Keller described alcoholism as an 'emotional illness'. Keller spent his career researching alcohol and its effect, defining alcoholism as excessive drinking — drinking in amounts affecting the drinker's health and/or their social or economic function. This is the definition which makes most sense to me as the daughter of an alcoholic.

◆

> *I can barely remember the poem, its words lost to the last years of my childhood. But its essence haunts me. There was a hallway, long and foreboding. Ears straining for the gentle closing of the door at the entrance, or its telling slam. A sky with dark grey clouds. A 'winterous' storm threatening to unleash.*

◆

I don't know when Dad's drinking became excessive. Was he already a 'drinker' before he left Italy? Did his drinking increase after he arrived in Australia? He couldn't speak the language at first, learning English while serving customers chunks of bratwurst, scoops of sauerkraut or pickles, and thin dark slices of pumpernickel bread in a German delicatessen. Six years later, at twenty-five, after a stint mining for opals in Coober Pedy, he was working in the drive through of the Arkaba Hotel where he met my then-sixteen-year-old mother who was helping take money on the door at raucous events playing Beatles music. Her mother encouraged her, saying how good he was to his own mother and therefore how good he'd be to her. He was already drinking heavily.

Mum said he seemed like fun at first, and she enjoyed his company. They quickly slipped into a routine, including lunch with his family once a week. He treated her well in those days. He was full of promises for their life together. When we get married... he'd say. But he was insecure. If she looked at a man, she was having an affair with him. This insecurity I remember well. It bordered on manipulative. If Mum went on a diet, Dad would be the 'romantic' husband and bring her a box of chocolates.

In the years after they met, there were drinks each night. Dad progressed to a flask of whisky in the pocket. He didn't hide his drinking, seeing nothing wrong with it. Mum worked her shifts as an apprentice hairdresser and later in her own salon. After dinner, they'd go to his delicatessen where they hand-peeled and sliced twenty kilos of potatoes for hot chips the next day. Mum soon discovered Dad wasn't interested in anything that wasn't work or drink. He wouldn't do anything fun or new. Years later, when our family went out on a walk, to a market, or for a drive in the Adelaide hills, Dad would stay home and potter around and sleep and drink.

◆

I see my dad in the backyard playing with us kids — just a random reel in my mind — when I was still little, maybe five or six. My big brother sits atop the tall monkey bars, my little brother on the swing. And I hang upside-down, my pigtails flapping below me as I show Dad my tricks. I see a happy family. Dad's playing with us kids. Mum's hanging washing on the line nearby. I feel the warmth of Dad's attention, see him proud of me, his little girl being a 'big girl'. Daddy's girl.

◆

Dad was diagnosed with diabetes when I was eight or nine. He would have been forty-three or four. Type 2 diabetes, the doctor said. Alcohol-induced diabetes. Didn't listen to the doctors when they told him to reduce his alcohol consumption. Instead, he found his own way. Rosé had been his wine of choice with its 6.25 grams of sugar in every 250ml glass. A glass of dry Riesling can have as little as 1.5 grams. It was the sugar causing his diabetes, Dad decided, not the drinking. He took away the Rosé but kept the Riesling. The alcohol content comparable across both wines at 12.5 to 13.5 percent remained the same.

◆

Dad loved broad beans boiled in salt water. He would shuck them one by one, leaving a pile of skins on his plate. Chestnuts, roasted in an open pan with holes in its base, each nut slit to avoid exploding. Sprinkles of salt on crunchy *finocchio,* which I didn't discover was called 'fennel' until my late teens. But these were occasional, seasonal offerings. Regular meals included large amounts of meat with crusty bread to lap up the juices or tomato *passata*. There were steaks and chops, sausages, schnitzels, and meat patties. Mum reminded me he also loved offal: kidney, liver, other giblets. I remember well the few times these were served to us kids and how they were pushed around our plates instead of being eaten. I turned vegetarian when I was twelve.

◆

There are numerous causal factors — traumas, relationship issues, loss and subsequent grief, etc. — in the progression from a first drink to one drink being that of many. But those factors don't affect everyone who takes a first drink.

There isn't anybody I can ask about when my father took his first drink. If he was from that moment hooked, or of it wasn't until after he left his home and his friends and came to Australia that alcoholism set in. I imagine him in his small home in the beachside village of Silvi Marina. I saw it once, in the middle of winter, when I was fourteen. It had recently been sold so I didn't get to see inside. By then the rectangular, white brick house was a street back from the beach, which couldn't be seen through the row of buildings set aside for tourists during the summer. In Dad's time his home would've been on the beachfront, without a busy road and buildings in between.

I see a large room with a table in the centre. Bedrooms off to one side. A kitchen dominated by a wood stove. A small store at the back selling fresh and dried fruits and vegetables, barrels of legumes, handmade spaghetti and pasta, fish straight from *Nonno's* ocean catch. Breads, cheeses, salami, which would fill their own lunchtime table, followed by steaming pasta in rich tomato sauce. In Italy, it was normal for children to drink some wine with their meal, and Dad would have seen his father drinking.

To me, Nonno, was the man in the corner of the room at my uncle's house. We would kiss him with a *Ciao* when we arrived, and there was another kiss and Ciao when we left. He was quiet. I don't remember him drinking. Mum said Nonno always had twenty litres of alcohol decanted into smaller bottles in the shed. Nonna, who also sat in the corner when we were there, held the keys to the shed, doling out the wine. Mum said you could tell when Nonno had had too much to drink as he rose from quiet to loud and argumentative. Dad was the same.

◆

Mum constantly tried to get Dad to eat better. She wanted him to eat more vegetables. Drink less. Keep on top of his sugar levels. Exercise.

He never listened to anyone, least of all Mum.

Mum always cooked 'meat and three veg', though I can't remember if she ever served any onto his plate. Meats, yes. Potato. Pasta, the meal of his childhood — freshly made when I was very young, in a pasta maker that pushed the dough through while I delighted in chopping the pieces of pasta as they reached the right length. My mum isn't Italian, but ooh... how she can cook, her skills way beyond my those of my Italian relatives.

When we hosted Christmas, Mum's talents would shine. I cannot fathom how she filled the Christmas table with so much festive food. Prawn cocktails first up, with a handmade sauce. Squares of her lavish lasagna, made with soft handmade crepes, layered with Napolitana or Bolognese sauce, zucchinis, carrots, eggplants, mozzarella and parmesan cheese, topped with more sauce and cheese, piping hot and ready to melt in your mouth. Bowls of peas, cooked with onion, sweet and juicy. Hasselback potatoes, drizzled in garlic or herbed butter; roasted pumpkin, carrots, onion and beetroot to go with the roasted chicken. For dessert, pavlova, puffed and decorated with whipped cream, strawberries, blueberries and kiwi fruit. Fruit cake. Sometimes a new creation such as chocolate mousse in chocolate shells, or mousse and cream filled brandy snaps. A caramel popcorn Christmas tree. Rounded bellies were topped off with strong, percolated coffee.

◆

Around three years ago, I wrote another poem about Dad. Though different and perhaps more mature than the one I wrote in my mid-teens, both poems share an essence. A foreboding. A fear that — I see in hindsight — permeated our home.

◆

Boxes of tomatoes at peak summer ripeness, boiled to a steaming juiciness, pushed through the tomato press, the thick juices splattering into repurposed fetta buckets until full. All day my family works, Dad boils the tomatoes and slops them into pots, Mum adds a handful of salt to each bucket and mixes it through. My brothers and I take turns turning the handle of the tomato press, pushing the juicy, bursting red balls through. My little sister flits around. My parents fill large brown beer bottles with hot sauce and cap them tight. Fresh, delicious passata ready for all-year-round lasagnas, pastas, soups, Dad's occasional treat of crabs in rich red sauce, stinking the house out all day as they cook. I remember that smell all these years later.

◆

Three years after my father died, I travelled to Italy and visited my Abruzzese cousins. I was sad we'd missed so much of each other's lives. Serious illness had knocked my cousins around, and when I visited, they were in their early sixties, me in my early forties. My cousin, Paulo, has since died, passing away quickly early last year. Iaia, his sister, died thirteen months later, in February this year. I was happy to connect with them, especially with Maria Rosaria (Iaia). We chatted with the help of google translate, yet when we got into a late night 'deep and meaningful' my Italian flowed and we spoke about how her mother struggled when her whole family left her behind in their home village with a new husband and two young children. I told my cousin what it was like growing up with my alcoholic father, and I enjoyed a half glass of wine with lunch, or after dinner a nip of limoncello, liquore liquiriza, or *nocello*, a delightful walnut and red wine liqueur made by Iaia. I savoured each wine, each spirit, let the flavours dance on my tongue, enhancing my experience of Iaia's delicious meals. For the first time, I enjoyed alcohol, knowing I'd never 'need' it as my dad did.

I didn't get to visit my dad's village on this occasion. It's winter, they said. A beachside village isn't a place to visit in winter. I promised to visit in the summer, a promise made just days before the world was locked down. Our summer together never came. I still want to walk the streets in the village near Dad's house, wander along the beach, feel the sand fall through my fingers, maybe pick up a shell to remind me of the trip. Watch the ocean and imagine my grandfather out there fishing, and though it will have changed since Dad was there, feel him in the place where he began.

◆

Mum remembers diabetes as one of the two main complications of my father's drinking while they were together. Impotence was the other, starting just before my sister was born when I was eight and a half. My mum didn't see the complications of Dad's failing body in later years, having divorced him when I was twenty-one. Dad's apathy and indifference finally broke apart the marriage and Mum left; the split I wish had happened years earlier occurred. Mum and my little sister went one way, my dad and little brother, who felt the need to support my father, the other.

In his last half a dozen years, we'd talk about his vegetable stews and other ways he was adding vegetables to his meals. Also, the smaller amount of meat he was eating. In reality, his body wasn't handling the richer foods anymore. In our twenty-minute phone calls each Sunday morning, it was something to talk about. But it was a case of 'too little, too late'. He was trying to reverse heart issues, sores on his legs and feet that wouldn't heal, the need for insulin by injection when he'd only used tablets before. All symptoms of long-term diabetes. He even had a little toe cut off; his legs so ulcerated he was lucky not to have lost more.

I don't know if he was still drinking then. I presume so.

◆

In the middle of the lounge room, there's a recliner chair. Dad's chair. A chair which when filled with its sleeping, snoring inhabitant, dominates not only the lounge room, but the dining room too, and the kitchen. Each night after dinner, we go to our rooms to do homework. Dad stays at the table reading the newspaper while finishing the last of his Riesling. We tiptoe down the stairs. If Dad's still at the table, we retreat, knowing that while he's awake, he might pick arguments with Mum, or she might say something that will set him off into tirades he won't remember in the morning.

If Dad's asleep, we know the way's clear and we can come down to watch TV or chat with Mum while he's laid out, fully reclined in the large green chair in the centre of the room. Though he can sleep through entire family evening activities, he doesn't always. So, we tip-toe around. I always wonder why he doesn't just go to bed.

On nights when my older brother's asthma becomes severe, Mum drags us three kids — before there are four — to the hospital, my older brother struggling to breathe. She doesn't dare leave us younger two alone with Dad asleep — comatose. If we were to wake up, he'd never know.

Back home after a night in Emergency, on waking, Dad doesn't know we left. He sleeps right through the drama of my brother's asthma attacks and Mum's given up telling him. He gets angry with Mum when she's tired the next day.

◆

the firebox

a metal box

glass front door

fire contained within

two flanking copper pots

filled with mallee roots

one to warm each night

dry roots

knobbly

a tonne more

in the shed

kindling

from broken produce boxes

once containing apples

pears

oranges, perhaps

white wood in broken shards

with a twist of the day's news

burst into flame

warm, cosy

sink into leather chairs

as Dad snores

sozzled on riesling or rosé

we tiptoe around him

dead to the world

yet awoken

by random noises

laughter

we go about our nights

as if he's not there

in his green recliner

in the centre of the room

demanding control

even in sleep

where rage bursts from

nothing

except the well-fuelled

spark of temper

in his head

◆

I felt shame around expressing my emotions, bursting into tears a lot when I was still very young., probably just like any other kid. My mum is more of a 'soldier on' kind of person, her favourite expression being 'Good soldiers don't look back'. She'd had her own traumas in childhood and married life certainly wasn't easy, so I can see why she chose, and still chooses, to focus on moving forward, leaving what has gone by alone.

I used to think Dad numbed his emotions, drank to feel blank, maybe. I wonder if he felt inferior somehow. Mum said he was anxious around authority figures. He'd smarten up his clothes, put on a nice shirt and make sure he shined his shoes before going to the doctor or even to a parent/teacher interview. Or avoid them altogether if he could. I see this anxiety in myself. I hibernate when I feel lacking in self-confidence. In those moments, I empathise with how Dad may have felt. I've even experimented with a drink or two to see if it helped. I didn't like the haziness it brought.

◆

Dad comes along to my dance concerts, right from when I'm young and into my teenage years. Mum encourages him to come, and I like to think he wants to be there to see me dance. He can't stay awake. I console myself — he's tired after working in the market all day. But it hurts. I want Dad to see me, like he did when I hung upside down on the swing, on the one time I remember.

◆

I went to a healer once, up in the northern suburbs of Sydney. A wonderful woman, Kim, who moonshined as a sound therapist from her usual days on the family cattle farm, four and a half hours north-east of the city. Somewhere, somehow, I think via kinesiology looking at childhood trauma, Kim came across some generational trauma, she said, on my father's side, four fathers back, so something passed down from my grandfather's grandfather. That the thread of addiction started beyond my father and grandfather makes sense. And if it did, what the hell happened to that man? He passed on a trauma that left a gnawing feeling in the men who came after. A feeling that needed to be numbed.

He would have been living in the mid-eighteen hundreds, right when the Risorgimento was happening, the unification of Italy. Or maybe it had something to do with Italy declaring war on Austria in 1866 – I have no records, but it's possible he went to war. Perhaps he was a victim of crime, or – we're talking Italy here – got caught up with the mafia. Or something more personal, betrayal or rejection, or loss of his first love. My ancestors were fishermen, possibly farmers too, living on Italy's Adriatic coast, right across the boot shaped country from Rome, which was declared the capitol of the Kingdom of Italy in 1870. The trials and traumas of this man, my great-great-grandfather, my nonno's nonno, aren't something I can ever know, but I feel for the man if the pain I see needing healing in his descendants is anything to go by.

◆

But my father wasn't an alcoholic – not in his mind. When questioned about his drinking habits, the doctor told him drinking in the morning was a sign of an alcoholic. My dad stopped adding brandy to his coffee. He wasn't an alcoholic.

◆

He's a storyteller and sometimes, though not often enough, he tells stories of his early adult years and his childhood, how he would follow his much older brother down the beach to shuck oysters from rocks. His stories tell of a carefree childhood, a simpler life. Like the time he wrestled a tortoise on the trip over from Italy. He never clarified how he came to be in the situation, so I'm left to imagine him jumping over the side of the boat on seeing the tortoise in the middle of who knows what ocean. He grabbed the tortoise and somehow got it back onto the ship and they all had tortoise stew while he kept the shell to hang on the wall of his future family home some twenty years later. Not likely. I like this persona, this strong, adventurous, capable young man he imagined for himself.

◆

We rarely get invited to visit with family friends. If we do, Dad drinks a whole bottle of their scotch. Even when they don't offer, he pesters until they dig out a bottle for him. We stay until the amber liquid's drained, then he snores in the passenger seat while Mum drives us home.

Weddings mean Dad causing a scene, loud and obnoxious, drunk beyond his usual measure. Once he almost gets run over as we go to the car. It's the norm. It's Dad. It's what he does. He's lucky, Mum says, there are no breathalysers in the mornings as he drives to work, most likely still over the limit. Maybe if he loses his license, she wonders — would that drive him to stop?

◆

Since 1785, when first defined, it has been debated whether alcoholism is a disease, or else a behavioural or moral issue. The first definition by Dr. Benjamin Rush explained intemperance as a disease and addiction. Other definitions, such as Dr. Magnus Huss's in 1849, point to alcoholism as a disease caused by excess alcohol consumption.

Alcohol brought truth. Dad used to say of his papa — in vino veritas est: in wine there's truth. Though he referred to the way his father would rant and rave when he drank, speaking what he considered the truth, alcohol also brought my father to life. Alcohol animated him. It brought out anger. Sometimes, in the early glasses, it brought out a jolly joy-like self. And it brought out a hurt that manifested in a mean streak, bringing down those around him as he told 'truths' about them, hurting them as perhaps he felt hurt inside.

Dad's drinking shows 'excess alcohol consumption' as a symptom, not a cause — although maybe it is causal in some people's experience.

◆

My parents fight. About his drinking, mostly. About my older brother who needs the firm hand of a father to tell him, No. I take on the protective role of my two younger siblings, often taking them down to the beach when my parents fight. I worry about Mum, not being able to protect her, not knowing if she's ok. And we never know when it's ok to return home.

In her book about addiction, It Will Never Happen to Me, which Mum took to reading, Claudia Black writes about how children in homes where addiction is present often get 'locked into roles based on their perception of what they need to do to survive and bring stability into their lives'. The propensity to over-protect both myself and anyone in my care has affected my home life and work relations as an adult. I tend towards attempting to create the stability that wasn't always present in my childhood, particularly my teenage years, by controlling situations and doing what I can to protect others in my care.

Black also writes about how siblings each cope in their own way and how it can affect their relationship with each other. I don't have overly close relationships with my siblings. I know my little brother remembers our trips to the beach as he mentioned them recently — the first time he's talked about anything from our childhood. I don't know about my sister — we don't talk about such things, or much at all, really. What really hurt was when we were cleaning out Dad's apartment and my older brother was pressing all my buttons, trying to trigger me and get me to leave. My younger siblings didn't do a thing to help. I don't think they even really registered what was going on, my older brother's behaviour being what we grew up with. I chose to leave — none of Dad's 'stuff' was worth the abuse. The hurt from my other siblings' lack of support remains.

◆

Again, I tried my hand at a poem, searching, trying to find my dad. This one differs, its essence sadder. A lone girl. A girl looking for her dad.

◆

In Australia, in the year starting mid-2017, the year Dad died, there were 191 million litres — 191 mega-litres — of pure alcohol available for consumption. That amount could fill seventy-six Olympic pools and allows for 10 litres of alcohol for each person over the age of fifteen each year. I assume figures were similar in proceeding years, give or take a swimming pool or two. While almost a quarter of Australian adults don't drink at all, another quarter drink what's considered an excess of over ten drinks a week or five drinks a day in any one month. Dad drank well beyond the excessive.

As I approach my mid-teens in the early nineties, Dad plays bowls across the road from our house, encouraged by Mum in her attempt to get him out socialising. My father, with his new friends, spends the early evening after his Wednesday afternoon bowls — other evenings, too — drinking in the club bar. My older brother works there and reports that Dad drinks a whole flagon of wine, at a measure of 2.25 litres, before trudging home late for dinner. On nights he stays in, he drinks from the cask he keeps in the cool room. This ginormous fridge in our large, purpose-built garage is there to keep stock cold for my parents' continental food shop. It's also the perfect place for Dad's cask of wine. Each glass, known by us as a 'fishbowl' for its round bowl-like shape, holds at least half a litre. Dad drinks two in a night and who knows how many out in the cool room in the fifteen minutes he takes to fill the glass.

So, if Dad drank, let's say, two litres each day, that'd mean in just four days he would have consumed a full litre of pure alcohol. I can hardly imagine such a potent liquid coursing through his system at such a volume. In just forty days, he would have drunk his entire 'share' of the country's alcohol, and over the year, that amount, nine times over. What it must have been doing to his insides, his liver, his brain. I know what it did to our family, and I'm still chipping away at what it did to me. I wonder how many children grow up, like me, seeing their father's or their mother's drinking as normal, yet the toxic substance their parent drinks erodes at the child's self-worth and sends them into adulthood feeling alone, when in fact they are one of many.

◆

A week and a half before Dad died, we spoke about his diabetes. I said something about never wanting to get diabetes. He said, You won't. You have a good diet. It was the first time he'd acknowledged my eating healthy was something positive. When I was twelve, my dad tried to force me to eat chicken after I'd become vegetarian (I couldn't bring myself to eat the animals I'd seen alive and running around one moment, heads flapping on broken necks the next, and on my plate that night). He pulled my ponytail, trying to make me eat. I was stuck in the chair where I ate every meal with Dad trying to push chicken into my mouth while painfully pulling my hair and me flailing around, trying to resist. Breaking free seemed impossible.

All those years later, in that moment on the phone, Dad gave me a little of the approval I'd sought from him as a child. It brought me some comfort, even if only in his dying days.

◆

walls

outside the bottle

i peer in:

dad

wrapped in glass

floats in a carafe of rosé

his rose-blurred glass

obscures me

hides him

in a riesling box

my dad

he hides:

packaged in silver

a plastic bladder

filled

sealed tight in his box

if i smash the glass

tear the cardboard

what

who

will i find?

a curl of a man

a foetal ball

hiding behind

those walls

Lucy Martinelli .Lucy Marinelli an Australian, Bali-based poet, creative writer and researcher with degrees in literature, creative writing and creative research. She conducts workshops internationally, and mentors poets and those seeking healing through poetry. Lucy spoke recently at the Asia Pacific Writers and Translators conference in Chang Mai and at the Singaraja Writers Festival. She's currently seeking publication for her poetry cycle, *The Rings From Your Fingers* and has written for *Swamp Online, Forbes WomenMedia, IN10, WA Poetry's Creatix,* and the big screens of the 2024 Perth Poetry Festival. Lucy's currently launching an online poetry community, *Poetic Light.*

Nureyev's Foot

Hsu-Ming Teo

There are many stories about pain and most of the published ones are heroic. This is not. This is an ugly story about pain. As ugly as Nureyev's foot.

There are two famous photographs of Rudolph Nureyev's bare foot *en pointe*. One is the black and white by Richard Avedon, the American photographer who specialised in fashion shoots, theatre, and dance. His 1961 portrait of the dancer is a sinuous ripple of light. Moody shadows slither over Nureyev's hairy, lower-right shin, drawing the eye down, across the furred and peeling heel to his over-arched sole, extended by an impossible 180 degrees. A grown man's body weight balanced on the blunt stubs of the first two toes. An unmanicured foot is a scaly gargoyle, fantastical and faintly absurd, bearing the scuffs and sufferings of life. In the hands of an artist like Avedon, the grotesquerie of Nureyev's foot transforms into grace, power, and a compellingly beautiful ugly.

The second portrait of Nureyev's foot was taken twenty years later by the Swiss photographer René Burri, when Nureyev danced the title role in the ballet *Manfred* in 1981. Burri's photo is less famous than Avedon's, or less frequently reproduced, at any rate. It shows a side view of the same section of the dancer's foot, bestial and forest-thick with hair and gnarly veins, clenched and unlovely. It is a stubborn wedge of tortured flesh with bones ripping through, anchored by the hard talon of the big toe. It is not a portrait of grace. It screams of pain.

Nureyev's foot is a visceral image of pain, the visual equipoise of unseen lives circling on a single point: the dancer and the other principals, the corps de ballet, the directors, choreographers, dancing masters, musicians, designers, costume makers, makeup artists, stagehands, ticket-sellers, and the many others—as well as their family, friends, and associates—whose livelihoods depend on his daily refusal to succumb to acute and chronic pain. A pain that must be hidden from view in the ballet shoe that transforms a claw into an *objet d'art* for the audience to admire.

It is different watching sports. We expect an athlete's performance in the arena of competition to include the outward display of inward pain: the rictus of a mouth scrunched into a grimace, the dramatic fall onto grass or court, palms clasped agonisingly over ankle or knee as the body, rocking, furls into foetal position. Spectators see these moments displayed up on the big screen, shot from various angles; it's part of the show. But on stage, a dancer's pain must be invisible, masked in fluid and unceasing movement. In her essay, 'Dancer and the Dance', Susan Sontag observes that 'the daily life of every dancer is a fulltime struggle against fatigue, strain, natural physical limitations and those due to injuries.' In every performance, she wrote, the dancer's smile is 'a categorical denial of what he or she is actually experiencing—for there is some discomfort, and often pain, in every major stint of performing.' The dancer's body tells a story of transcendence over flesh and triumph over pain.

Everybody has stories of pain. The literary scholar Elaine Scarry suggests that pain is intrinsically related to language, but that it also reveals the limitation of words. While fiction is replete with characters experiencing psychological and emotional distress, physical pain defies language and representability. Virginia Woolf wrote that 'English, which can express the thoughts of Hamlet and the tragedy of Lear, has no words for the shiver or the headache.'

And yet, pain is most effectively communicated to others through stories. Without narrative, the pain of others cannot be grasped, felt, and acted upon. How can we empathise with the body in agony without a story of origins and symptoms mediated through similes, metaphors and analogies, or metricised on a scale of one to ten? Especially when pain is internal and we cannot see its signs except perhaps in a grimace or shudder. So we recount our experiences of suffering as a way of bringing some measure of understanding, and even relief. We want to communicate our pain and we want to be heard. As physician and literary scholar Rita Charon comments, 'medicine has begun to affirm the importance of telling and listening to the stories of illness.'

Stories about pain follow the conventions of different genres; they have narrative arcs that often end with some kind of message. There is the genre of tragedy, where pain is destructive, socially isolating and alienating, diminishing the plenitude of an individual life to the lumpen flesh of the tortured body. 'You are a little soul carrying about a corpse,' wrote Marcus Aurelius in his *Meditations*. Then there's the modernist, nihilistic story where pain is ultimately meaningless; it simply is. There is also the genre that David B. Morris in *The Culture of Pain* calls 'postmodern pain', where there are many often clashing and contradictory meanings to pain experienced simultaneously or sequentially; meanings shaped by different cultural and historical contexts.

Most commonly, however, there is the romantic narrative of pain, where the hero's journey with and through pain is transformative and redemptive, if not always triumphant. Pain, or caring for someone in pain, calls us out of the world of the ordinary into harrowing adventure. On this journey, we often reach what Canadian literary scholar Northrop Frye calls the 'point of ritual (or, in the case of terminal illness, literal) death', where it seems there is nothing left to live for. But slowly, gradually, we fight our way to revelation. We return to the ordinary world, perhaps not healed but certainly transformed and, Prometheus-like, carrying for the benefit of others a fire-torch of hope. This is the inspirational story that becomes a bestseller and gets made into a Hollywood movie. This is the genre that shows us in our best light; it's the way most of us, I suspect, wish and hope we would be in our stories of pain.

This is the Nureyev story. In 1978, the renowned Russian cellist Mstislav Rostropovich urged the dancer to tell the story of Byron's *Manfred* in dance, choreographed to Tchaikovsky's symphony based on the same work. Nureyev loved the idea. His ballet premiered at the Paris Opera in November 1979, but instead of dancing the role of the tormented Manfred, Nureyev watched from the sidelines; he had broken a metatarsal in his foot dancing onstage a fortnight earlier in West Berlin. But he was out of his plaster cast and at the barre before the end of the month, practising intensely and pushing through the agony of barely healed bones. On 15 December 1979, six weeks after his injury, he danced the titular role at the Paris Opera for the first time. Two years later, he danced *Manfred* in Zürich and René Burri immortalised his ugly foot transcendent over pain. Nureyev's story is always narrated as a heroic story.

But this is not Nureyev's story. It is an ugly story about the women in my family who are designated the role of Nureyev's Foot: the point on which the weight of the whole family bears down and is sustained. Often in need of care themselves, they are expected to look after the rest of the family because, in the hierarchy of needs within the family, they are lowly ranked. They do not have priority because they are single women.

In 2022, when I myself was in great physical pain, I came up with what I thought was a clever idea to write about the pain of caregiving. I live with constant pain radiating from my neck down to my slightly deformed left foot. I was a figure-skater from the age of fourteen to forty-two. That's twenty-eight years of countless falls on the ice, sprains, pulled tendons, stress fractures, battered spine, hip joint and other injuries from thousands of hours of spins and jumps. A recent study by Brigham Young University sports scientists showed that when skaters land a jump, they exert around eight times their body weight on the ball of the foot within 50 to 125 milliseconds—a tremendously jarring force for the foot to absorb and distribute up the leg. In the long term, many skaters suffer from ongoing pain along the spine and hips. In my case, an ill-fitting boot caused two metatarsal bones in my left foot to collapse as well.

There's no point in trying to describe the pain I feel because there are no words to do so, and in any case, many people already understand this pain. If you tell almost anybody you have back pain, they will tell you they experience it too, and they will then proceed to tell you a story about their back pain, the various therapists and remedies they've tried, discuss whether acupuncture works, and even demonstrate for you the kinds of exercises you should be doing every day to alleviate your pain. Back pain is excruciating, and it's common, and nobody wants to hear another story about it. Even the sufferer can find talking about back pain more infuriating than therapeutic.

My idea, then, was not to write about my body in pain, but to write about trying to do my job and provide care for my ageing parents while in pain. In my self-conception back then, I was the embodiment of Nureyev's Foot: overlooked and unappreciated, but heroic somehow. I juggled running a large university department and struggling to meet my own teaching, research and writing deadlines with caregiving responsibilities. I looked after a father with Alzheimer's and a rather helpless mother who had grown increasingly resentful against her irascible husband. Her frustration no doubt came from a mess of grief and thwarted expectations over many decades of a loving but unhappy marriage. Her feelings provoked a corresponding rage and twisting grudge in me that, as a supposedly filial daughter, I was not supposed to feel. I have usually been competent and reliable as a caregiver, though not always pleasant about it. Through my own choice, since I always knew I'd be the one to take care of them in their old age, I lived five minutes away from my parents. I was at their beck and call. All this I did, not without significant resentment, but also with a conceited martyr's air of self-sacrificial purpose. After all, this was the role I had been brought up to fulfil; a role first designated to my Auntie Wan-Ting,[5] my godmother and surrogate mother.

Auntie Wan-Ting is the archetypal Nureyev's Foot in my mother's Singaporean family. Despite being the youngest of my mother's eight siblings,[6] my Chinese grandmother on her deathbed entrusted the care of her husband and the family to Auntie Wan-Ting. This is unusual in Chinese families because in Confucian culture, it is the duty of the eldest sibling—not the youngest—to care for the family. But the eldest sister had migrated to the UK, while another sister had married and left for Hong Kong. My mother also married and moved away—first to Malaysia in 1966, then to the UK in 1972, back to Malaysia a year later,

---

[5] All names have been changed in this essay. The characters in the female name Wan-Ting (婉婷) are associated with grace and gentleness.

[6] My mother is technically one of twelve siblings but one died as a baby, another was adopted to another relative, and her father later adopted his brother's eldest son as his own eldest son. She, the fifth child, only counts the eight she grew up with as her siblings. Yes, it's complicated.

and finally, with three children in tow, to Australia in 1977. Auntie Wan-Ting remained in Singapore. She got a job at a bank in Singapore, looked after my grandfather until his death in 1972, and thereafter fulfilled her designated role as the anchor of my mother's family, connecting the siblings and their children—my cousins—to each other.

On a steamy afternoon in late 1978, when grumbling thunderheads massed low in a steel-grey sky, Auntie Wan-Ting was summoned from work to inspect the remains of a body mashed into the pavement outside an apartment block in Singapore. Her second eldest sister had jumped off the rooftop. To this day, she mainly remembers the rotting stench of blood, pulpy brains and ruptured guts. She dealt with the police and comforted the family. It was expected of her, and she expected it of herself. She'd made a promise to her mother, and by that time she also worked as a part-time pastor in an Anglican church. It was her job to suck it up and see to the needs of others.

The griefs of a single woman, and the youngest in the family at that, were of little interest. It wasn't that her siblings did not love her; absorbed in their own family dramas, they simply saw her through the prism of their yawning need. She became the family counsellor, and the source of financial aid when one uncle gambled away his house, when another uncle died leaving his widow and four children with little support, and when my mother needed a loan to pay taxes on her dental practice.

She kept secrets well, perhaps because she had no-one in whom to confide. Singapore had survived a vicious three-and-a-half-year occupation by the Japanese army during World War II, the clash between British armed forces and Chinese communist guerillas during the Malayan Emergency of 1948 to 1960, decolonisation, expulsion from the federated states that constituted Malaysia, the achievement of independence and the subsequent task of consolidating a multiracial city-state. The country was resolutely focused on the future. It was not, at that time, a society in which stories of trauma were encouraged or understood. So when she was raped by a flatmate, humiliation and fear kept her silent until, when I was fourteen and visiting Singapore for the first time since my family migrated to Australia, she shared her secret with me. I had confided that I was sexually assaulted at the age of eleven, pulled off my bike after taking a shortcut through a sunny but deserted alley on my way to Strathfield library to return a bag of books. I too told nobody but her; my childhood home—where the duties of love intermingled daily with bellowed accusations and the stench of disappointment—was a place of terror for me. The prospect of incurring my father's wrath yet again (*why had I taken the shortcut to the library!*) and the reflexive sense of culpability instilled in a child brought up to assume responsibility for everything kept me silent. We were bonded by our shared shame.

My childhood ticked away to the metronomic beat of Auntie Wan-Ting's woes. I learned that Auntie Wan-Ting had joined the Anglican church as a full-time pastor, only to get kicked out when she uncovered financial wrongdoing. She lost her government-designated apartment, then had her foot run over by a careless motorcyclist and was wheelchair bound for a time, told that she might never walk again. But if her family was not there to care for her or even to visit regularly, she nevertheless had a treasure in her best friend Kwong-Ming, whom she met in the late 1980s and with whom she later shared a home by the 1990s. It was Kwong-Ming (another single Chinese woman who was the Nureyev's Foot of her own family—but that's a different story) who wheeled Auntie Wan-Ting everywhere so that she might not be housebound, and who forced her through the agony of rehabilitation exercises that she might learn to walk again. Over time, Auntie Wan-Ting's congenital issues—an unusually small heart with inadequately formed blood vessels—were compounded by stress, other injuries, and multiple problems affecting her eyes, liver, spine, hands, and the neural connections in her brain. Despite her deteriorating health, she remained Nureyev's Foot for her family: the first phone call in the middle of the night when trouble came, the first to provide counsel, comfort or cash.

In 2020, a decade after Kwong-Ming's death, Auntie Wan-Ting opened her apartment and provided hospice care for her cancer-stricken cousin, Lina, when Singapore was in a government-mandated 'circuit breaker lockdown' during the coronavirus pandemic. My Auntie Lina had also been a Nureyev's Foot to her own family. Single and successful, she doted on her late brother's children and looked after her own mother with the same simmering anger and resentment I'm dismayed to recognise in myself. Like my mother, hers also favoured sons over daughters. Having expended all her love, time, energy and income on her mother and nieces and nephews, Auntie Lina reached the end of her life only to find that, in her debilitated state, she was an unwanted burden to the family. Her brother did not wish to look after her, claiming he could not care for both his mother and his sister. Her nieces, one a surgeon and the other an actuary, claimed they were too busy with work. Nobody wanted to pay for her to move into a hospice, so she moved into Auntie Wan-Ting's spare bedroom to die, looked after to the end by my aunt and her Filipina caregiver (yet another Nureyev's Foot for her own family back in Laoag in The Philippines). But there are no heroes in this ugly story of pain. Auntie Lina, unable to admit that the family to whom she had devoted her life was unwilling to care for her, turned her rage on Auntie Wan-Ting and the Filipina caregiver, abusing them both. It was a relief when she finally died.

This June, Auntie Wan-Ting's caregiver has to return to The Philippines for a month to commemorate the one-year anniversary of her mother's death. Auntie Wan-Ting cannot be left alone for long because of her health issues and her propensity to have accidents when her motor neurons abruptly stop connecting with her muscles, which happens from time to time. But as with Auntie Lina, there is no sibling, nephew or niece in Singapore who is willing or able to tend to this Nureyev's Foot, so I'll step up and do it.

I don't want this designated role of Nureyev's Foot, although I'm afraid my mother sees it as my legacy since she gave me to Auntie Wan-Ting as her goddaughter. When I first had the idea for this essay, the thought of Nureyev's Foot and what it represents choked me with panic. I did not—and still do not—know how to juggle long hours of work with looking after my parents in Sydney and looking after my godmother in Singapore.

Lately, though, it occurs to me that I've got this wrong. I haven't told the whole story of Nureyev's foot.

After he broke his foot in West Berlin, Nureyev was determined that the premiere of *Manfred* should not be delayed, just as he was equally determined that he would perform the ballet at the Paris Opera before it closed in the new year. He had no time for self-pity. Instead, he cast Jean Guizerix and Michael Denard as his stand-ins and showed up to rehearsals every day to direct them, wrapped in brightly striped sweaters and baggy brown corduroy pants, stomping around in heavy felt slippers, leaning slightly on his elegant silver-headed cane, those piercing grey eyes sweeping the stage from under the visor of his brown fur cap. He knew he was not irreplaceable, and he knew that one day it would all come to an end. 'Nature is clever about these things,' he said to the *New York Times* journalist Flora Lewis in 1979. 'I'll dance as long as I enjoy it. When it becomes painful, I will find it unpleasant and be dissatisfied.' As his body broke down, he turned his energy to directing and choreographing ballets, and even conducted orchestras for ballet performances.

I started writing this piece egotistically imagining myself as Nureyev's Foot—the fulcrum of the family. It was a role that aggravated and embittered me as much as it gave me a sense of self-importance. But in the course of writing this essay, I have come to realise two things: first, that the dancer is replaceable, and second, that the photo of the foot is only significant because of the name attached to it. Without the name 'Nureyev', the foot becomes any old dancer's gnarled and ugly foot, still wondrous, still miraculous, still a scream of pain—but of interest to very few.

I am replaceable as a caregiver. When I fly to Singapore in June to look after Auntie Wan-Ting, my brother and sister-in-law will take centre stage in the choreography of my parents' care. Indeed, if only I had not been so absorbed in presenting myself as Nureyev's Foot, I might have seen that they have always been part of the dance. I was never the star, the principal dancer. I was just another member of the corps de ballet who took a turn as the principal for a time. By attaching the name 'Nureyev' to this tale, I have tried to give it a gravitas and significance it perhaps did not need or deserve, for what I do, what I have described in this story, is simply ordinary. Millions of people do this every single day, and we do it because we love. How utterly extraordinary.

My heartfelt thanks to Michael Campbell for insisting that I write 'the ugly story', and to Kim Swivel and Michelle Hamadache for their insightful feedback.

Hsu-Ming Teo is Professor of Literature and Creative Writing, and the former Head of the Department of Media, Communications, Creative Arts, Language, and Literature (MCCALL) at Macquarie University. Her first novel *Love and Vertigo* (2000) won *The Australian*/Vogel Literary Award and was shortlisted for several other awards. Her second novel *Behind the Moon* (2005) was shortlisted for the NSW Premier's Literary Awards.

ACKNOWLEDGMENTS

This book would not be possible without the vision, wisdom, encouragement, and support of Michael Campbell, Executive Director and Publishing Director of WestWords. Michael, we are truly grateful for your invaluable contributions to creative writing at Macquarie University over the years. Our partnership is one we treasure.

Our thanks to the former Department of Media, Communications, Creative Arts, Languages, and Literature (MCCALL) at Macquarie University for funding the initial project meetings. We are especially grateful to the following colleagues from MCCALL for their insightful presentations on writing ethically about illness and disability: Associate Professor Nicole Matthews, Associate Professor Kate Rossmanith, and Dr Jessica Kirkness. Jessica, along with Associate Professor Willa McDonald, also volunteered time, experience and expertise mentoring student writers on the project.

A big thank you also goes to Tedi Symons and Lili Watkins-Murphy, Macquarie Higher Degree Research students whose work on the project was invaluable.

This Macquarie University project was conceived and developed on the land of the Wallumattagal People of the Dharug Nation, whose customs, cultures, and stories have nurtured and enriched this land since time immemorial. We acknowledge and pay our respects to Elders and all Aboriginal people, past and present, who established a flourishing tradition of storytelling in this country. We honour these traditions and achievements, and follow in these footsteps with humility.

Professor Hsu-Ming Teo and Dr Michelle Hamadache

Professor Hsu-Ming Teo
Former Head of the Department of Media,
Communications, Creative Arts, Languages
and Literature (MCCALL)
Macquarie University

Dr. Michelle Hamadache
Director of Creative Writing, Discipline
of English and Creative Writing,
School of Humanities, Faculty of Arts,
Macquarie University

THANK YOU

This project was made possible by the generous donations who supported the project through the Australian Cultural Fund.

They are: Heather Austin, Sarah Bolger, Yazmín Bradley, Barton Green, Erin McFadyen, Seth Molinari, Jenny Packer, Brett Perry, Pamela Ramsden, Karen Roberts, Peter Skinner, Thomas Skinner, Vivienne Skinner, Joshua Taylor, Mardi Taylor, Hsu-Ming Teo, Judith Vran, Bryony Walters and four further anonymous donations. We thank you for bringing these stories into these pages so they can be shared, fostering a deeper understanding and empathy of those living with chronic illness and disability.

Chronic Pain Australia

Chronic Pain Australia is the national voice for people living with chronic pain. As a not-for-profit, consumer-led organisation, it works to reduce stigma, improve access to care, and build a supportive community for the 1 in 5 Australians affected by ongoing pain. Through advocacy, education, and peer support, Chronic Pain Australia helps individuals feel seen, heard, and empowered. *www.chronicpainaustralia.org.au*

10% of book sales will go to Chronic Pain Australia